EDUCATION AND HUMAN RESOURCE DEVELOPMENT

EDUCATION AND HUMAN RESOURCE DEVELOPMENT

By

Dr. M. Lakshmi Narasaiah

M.A., Ph.D.

Professor of Economics,
Coordinator, Department of M.B.A.
Sri Krishnadevaraya University Post-graduate Centre,
Kurnool–518 002
Andhra Pradesh (India)

DISCOVERY PUBLISHING HOUSE
NEW DELHI

Edition - 2016

ISBN: 978-81-7141-928-9

Education and Human Resource Development

Published by:

DISCOVERY PUBLISHING HOUSE PVT. LTD.
4383/4B, Ansari Road, Darya Ganj
New Delhi-110 002 (India)
Phone: +91-11-23279245, 43596064-65
Fax: +91-11-23253475
E-mail: discoverypublishinghouse@gmail.com
sales@discoverypublishinggroup.com
web: www.discoverypublishinggroup.com

Printed at:
Infinity Imaging Systems
Delhi

Preface

In contrast to the food supply challenge posed by the coming wave of population growth, the global need for teachers and classrooms will rise very slowly in the next half-century. In many countries, the school-age population is increasing much less rapidly than the overall national population, the trend illustrates that growth rates typically differ for different age strata of the population. It also shows that declining birth rates can take decades to move through an entire population.

At the global level, for example, total population is projected to increase by 54 per cent between 2000 and 2050, but the number of children aged 5 to 14 will grow by only 6 per cent. And of the world's largest countries—accounting for 60 per cent of global population in 1995—will actually begin to see decreases in the number of children aged 5 to 14 by 2015; for several of these countries, the decline in this age group has already begun. These countries will need fewer classrooms and teachers to educate the youngest members of society (assuming they maintain current class size and student-teacher ratios).

Plenty of nations, however, still have increasing child-age populations. Where countries have not acted to stabilize population, the base of the national population, pyramid continues to expand, and pressures on the educational system will be severe. In the world's 10 fastest-growing countries, for example, most of which are in Africa and the Middle East, the child-age population will increase in average 93 per cent over the next half-century. Africa as a whole will see its school-age population grow by 75 per cent through 2040.

The rapid growth in African population is especially worrisome because of the extra burden it imposes in a region already lagging in education. Only 56 per cent of Africans south of the Sahara are literate, compared with 71 per cent for all developing countries. Few African countries have universal primary education, and secondary education reaches only 4-5 per cent of African children. Educating today's children is challenge enough; the addition of another three students for every four already there will require heroic investments in education. But the alternative is grim: without additional investments in education, today's average student-teacher ratio of 42 in sub-Saharan Africa will reach 75 by 2040.

Many countries will be challenged to increase funding for education while ensuring that other worthy sectors also receive the support they need. With 900 million illiterate adults in the world, the case for a renewed commitment to education is easy to make. But competing for these funds are the 840 million chronically hungry and the 1.2 billion without access to a decent toilet.

The budget stresses on governments attempting to meet these basic needs would clearly be reduced with smaller populations. Mozambique and Lesotho, for example, both met the UNESCO benchmark for investment in education in 1992-6 per cent of gross domestic product—and the two countries economies were roughly equal in size. Yet because Mozambique has many times the population of Lesotho, spending per child in Lesotho is about nine times higher than in Mozambique. For the majority of countries who do not meet the UNESCO funding standard, many of whom also fall short in providing other basic services, a decline in population pressure could help substantially to meet all of their social goals.

If national education systems begin to stress life-long learning for a rapidly changing world, as recommended by a 1998 UNESCO report on education in the twenty-first century, then extensive provision for adult education will be necessary, affecting even those countries with shrinking childgage populations, Such a development means that countries that started population stabilisation programmes earliest will be in the best position to educate their entire citizenry.

Dr. M. Lakshmi Narasaiah

Contents

1

Promotion of Higher Education in Research

The central role of Universities in the development of skills and knowledge as an absolute prerequisite for national development is un-disputed. Higher education institutions have the responsibility for training a country's high level professional, technical and managerial personnel, they are to generate new knowledge through research and advanced scientific training, and they serve as agents in the transfer, adaptation and dissemination of knowledge. Higher education institutions also play an important role in contributing to the social cohesiveness of a nation and as a forum for constructive debates on development.

In a world economy which is heavily science-based and technology-driven higher education institutions, and particularly universities, have to provide such a competence which is indispensable for building a country's endogenous capacity for problem identification and problem solution through education combined with research. In India, however, universities have so far not been able to fulfil these roles, partly because the multiplicity of their missions is hardly compatible. Many critics of the universities in India consider them to be institutions of learning and research separated from the main stream of the economic and social needs of the population which they are supposed to serve. Most of them have not managed to reconcile the missions of providing country-oriented training and research and of being part of a wider international scientific community. Higher education institutions in many countries all over the world are confronted with a large scale and mostly uncontrolled expansion of the higher education sector and the concomitant growth expenditure against a background of dwindling financial resources to support such expansion. As a result of this expansion the quality of teaching and research has declined due to overcrowding, inadequate staffing, poor physical facilities and equipment. In addition universities often show a poor capacity for management and administration. This results in a low internal efficiency which amongst others is responsible for a rising graduate under or unemployment.

These deficiencies and a lack of national resources produce dependence on external sources particularly for research development. The low capacity for planning and management makes it difficult to properly employ external sources so that there may be pockets of good quality research in one field unrelated to neighbouring areas and not forming part of an endogenous research tradition.

Measures to be Taken

The measures may be aimed specifically at increasing the efficiency of the system of higher education or of individual institutions by improving development relevance, quality and performance. More specifically are:

- to optimise and diversify the structure in line with the country's development requirements;
- to improve the capacity for efficient planning and administration;
- to diversify funding sources, with the aim of relieving the state budget;
- to improve access for talented students from all segments of society, giving special attention to the proportion of women studying.

At the level of individual institutions of higher education the aim should be improve

- education and training performance in the academic-scientific and vocational field;
- research and development capacities, especially in applied fields;

- the capacities to provide constancy and services to contractors in state, business and industry, and society.

In order to achieve these objectives, it is necessary

- to train the academic, administrative and technical staff,
- to improve the infrastructure including central facilities and means of communications and
- to increase efficiency by improving organisation.

The concept stresses the importance of measures designed to increase the efficiency of higher education in general through the strengthening of management capacities both at the system and at the institutions levels. This extends, inter alia, to the diversification of institutions of higher education in line with development needs, diversification in terms of funding, (including cost-sharing through fees) diversification in terms of study courses and practice-oriented training offered. Academic training at different levels for technical and executive staff.

New Areas of Promotion

The promotion of higher education institutions and subjects considered relevant for development (agriculture, natural sciences, engineering, medicine), the revised concept has to include areas such as the protection of the environment and resources, education, family planning and population policy.

In the wake of the political and economic reorientation taking place in many countries subjects like economics, law and social sciences are increasing in importance.

Prospects

Each country needs capacities which can produce the necessary analytical competence and research for generating information needed for designing and monitoring its development path. Institutions of higher education are essential in providing this competence. The responsibility for advanced education and the production of ideas and information should not be left to external donors. This may entail the concentration of resources, both internal and external, on one or only a few institutions of a country.

2

Will Education Go to Market?

The World Trade Organisation has launched processes that could open up to competition the expanding and highly protected world market in education. What issues are at stake? Mot of us see education as first and foremost a public service which is responsible for providing young people with instruction. For investors looking for somewhere to put their money it is also an annual budget of $1,000 billion worldwide, a sector employing 50 million people, and above all a billion potential customers in the form of students.

The decision to extend services the liberalisation of international trade which previously applied to commodities was taken in 1994. The General Agreement on Trade in Services (GATS) which was signed in April of that year included education on the list of services to be liberalised. To say outside the scope of this agreement a country's education system must be completely financed and administered by the state, which is no longer the case anywhere. However, each country can still decide freely what commitments it wants to make, and especially which educational sectors it wants to expose to market forces. The New Zealand government, for example, has decided to open up to outside competition the whole private education sector, from primary to university level.

So far, New Zealand is an exception, but that situation is likely to change. Part 4 of the GATS agreement ("Progressive liberalisation") requires that fresh negotiations should be held by the end of 2000 at the latest, and should be directed to "the elimination of the adverse effects on trade in services of measures as a means of providing effective market access". At the Geneva headquarters of the World Trade Organisation (WTO), far from the headlines and the demonstrators, work still goes on. But independently of the WTO and national policies, a number of factors are diving educational systems towards "communication".

Pressures for Change

First, education is a rapidly-growing sector in which governments are finding it harder and harder to satisfy demand, above all in higher education. Between 1985 and 1992, the number of students in higher education rose about 26 per cent—from 58.6 to 73.7 million. Meanwhile, public spending on education has tended to stagnate over the past 15 years (5-6 per cent of GDP in rich countries and 4 per cent else where).

In view of this dearth of public spending, parents and students are increasingly looking to private education for a solution. In the United States, every episode of violence in a state school and every scandal that rocks official school systems gives a boost to "home schooling", where children no longer attend school and are taught at home.

Traditional public education is also coming in for strong criticism. Employers complain it is not geared to their needs and is not flexible enough. Under pressure from economic interests, a process of "deregulating" education system has begun. The growing independence of schools is encouraging them to look for alternative sources of funding, ranging from sponsorship to full management by private companies and including many kinds of partnerships between schools and firms. The time for out-of-school education has come... the liberalisation of the educational process thereby made possible will lead to control by education service providers who are more innovative than the traditional structures.

The development and spread of information and communication technologies on a massive scale make possible the development of paid distance learning, using multimedia and the Internet for tutorials, examinations, etc.

Secondary and primary education are also affected. More and more paying Internet sites bill themselves as alternatives to state schools or traditional private schools. The computer screen takes over from the teacher, for a fee of around $2,250 a year.

The WTO secretariat set up a working group in 1998 to look at prospectus for more liberalised education. Its report pointed to the rapid growth of distance learning and noted the increasing number of partnerships between educational institutions and private firms.

Education for Export

Some 350 U.S. experts on international trade in services, including 170 businessmen and women, gathered at the U.S. Commerce Department in Washington on October 16, 1998 to draw up recommendations for the U.S. negotiators at the WTO. The purpose of the meeting, called Services 2000, was to look at how the U.S. government should continue to support the efforts of American business to take competitive advantage in foreign markets". The US currently controls about 16 per cent of the world market in services. Its services exports have more than doubled in the past 10 years and now cover 42 per cent of the non-services trade deficit.

The United States is also the world's leading exporter of educational services, and a working group at the Services 2000 conference paid special attention to this sector. It concluded that the sector "needs the same degree of transparency, transferability and interchangeability, mutual recognition, and freedom from undue regulation or restraints and barriers that the United States acknowledges on behalf of other service industries". The report said that three points should be at the centre of WTO negotiations about education.

Firstly, there should be a free flow of electronic information and means of communication, nationally and internationally. Secondly, the negotiators should tackle "barriers and other restrictions that limit or prevent the provision of educational and training services across countries and internationally." They were also to deal with obstacles to the transferability of degree and diplomas.

Fighting for Market Share

The U.S. demands are backed by most countries of the APEC (Asia-Pacific Economic Cooperation) zone. In a note in October 1999, the Australian delegation to the WTO said it would be "encouraging all members to make expanded commitments in all sectors, even the ones that have proved difficult in both regional and multilateral services negotiations", particularly education.

South Korea took a similar position. At a meeting of ministers of Human Resources from APEC Countries that it hosted in September 1997, the Seoul government put out a memorandum which clearly stated its vision of education as a tool of economic competition.

"The emphasis on education for itself or on education for good members of a community without a large emphasis on preparation for future work is no longer appropriate. Such a view of education and work cannot be justified in a world where economic development is emphasised.

"At present, in many economies, the education system do not sufficiently reflect labour market conditions. Their inflexible and inefficient education systems could not meet the new economic environmental challenges." So education should be made more "flexible", i.e. be deregulated and liberalised. In particular, "School systems should be established to allow all students to study what they are interested in "and "employers, with school educators, should share the role of educating students".

Some think resistance to liberalizing education will come from Europe, especially France. "The future WTO negotiations cannot call in question France's tradition of public service in the field of education and health", stressed a report on the WTO.

3

Corporate Ambitions in Education

Centralisation and efficiency, frequently invoking the powerful metaphor of scientific management or "Taylorism," using the stopwatch and management to discover the "one best way." These principles had been instrumental, industrialists of the time believed, in creating the industrial revolution and the wealth of powerful international companies. The quest for efficiency of those decades led to the problems we must now repair, notably the rigid and bureaucratic structure of our school systems.

Today, public schools continue to adapt new business efficiency techniques in what seems to be a constant recycling process. Scientific management, it turns out, was only the precursor to a host of ever newer management theories aimed at encouraging greater worker productivity and hence greater national wealth.

When Schools Become Levers to Attract Business Investment

These trends have echoes in the management reforms prescribed for and adopted by schools. Some seek increased efficiency through decentralised school governance while others image that outsourcing (or contracting) the management and operation of schools will lift educators' performance because incentives are lacking in secure government jobs.

All this is happening against the backdrop of economic globalisation, which inevitably creates political tensions by pitting governments against one another in competition for transnational corporate jobs and global capital. Our current era mimics the turn of the century to the extent that international capital flows and transnational production processes influence both corporation and governments. Today, technologically induced speed, growth among investors, concentration of wealth, and interconnectedness have increased the effects of this global speculation and decreased the capacity of governments to regulate business and markets. Not surprisingly, this global market ideology has been broadly recognised as a force in national education policy.

Reforming local schools becomes one of the ways that cities engage in the global competition to provide production resources to corporations. When formal schooling is seen as a key element of productive capacity, a view reinforced by the decline of manufacturing and the rise of information-based technologies, the quality of the local public school system takes on renewed importance for business leaders and local politicians alike. Today's corporate leaders have uncommon access to elect political officials and government agency heads, the wealth of large corporations to draw upon, and the ability to affect local and regional economics simply by making business decisions.

Schools are treated as engines of economic development to lure business to a particular city or state, so corporate and local political leaders corporate in their governance and redesign. In short, school policy becomes labour policy?

This powerful combination of corporate, national and state executives is happening at the expenses of education professionals. In contrast to the turn of the century, when educators played a pivotal role in debates by emphasising the role of schools in developing citizenship, today they have been largely discredited. Selecting school leaders from outside the field has become both symptom and spur to this decrease in the educator's status. A small but influential group of school districts is choosing leaders from among the ranks of businessmen, politicians and the military, rather than educators.

All this is taking place with little evidence that recent management solutions will turn around poor schools, nor that improvements in school performance protect against declines in productivity or the business cycle. Yet there are more troubling problems with reform strategies that pit the market against government in education. One is that education is reduced to its narrowest economic purposes. According to a 1992 survey, corporate executives most want schools to emphasize "a basic understanding of math and science:" and "sound work habits such as self-discipline, timeliness and dedication to work." These are laudable goals, but reflect a narrow set of traits that employers predict their workers will need in an information economy.

The corporate model of reform pays little heed to other expectations of public schools: building just and tolerant communities, reducing distrust of one another and our shared institutions, safe guarding democratic ethics and introducing children to the cultural wisdom of the world. We are also witnessing the abandonment of many kinds of equality. Neither markets nor business ethics routinely put equality or fairness above profits. Whole groups of people will not fit the prevailing model of what it takes to be competitive in an educational market place in which competition is the guiding principle of improvement. Another disturbing trend is the anaemic citizenship that economic justifications for schooling envision. Increasing the emphasis on individualism is likely to exacerbate a pattern of civic disengagement many already find disturbing in its scale and scope.

A Balancing Act to Reach a Healthy Equilibrium

We need a contemporary counter-movement to restore a healthy equilibrium of goals for our public schools. This movement would be grounded in a very different educational critique that rejects the metaphor of market (or management) failure and instead tackles the problems in our schools as symptoms of a widespread civic breakdown. The solutions to school failure would then hinge on common concerns, rather than rigorous individual competition and accountability. In addition to academic criteria parents and reformers would craft student performance measures that reward active citizenship, tolerant and respectful behaviour, and cultural knowledge in the arts, history and languages. This reform movement, seeking equity and tolerance, would revitalize democratic institutions and not merely aim for more efficient production.

4

Private Education: *The Poor's Best Chance?*

Across the developing world, private schools and education companies are not only flourishing, but reaching the poor. India is a case in point. A Common assumption about the private sector in education is that it caters only to the elite, and that its promotion only serves to exacerbate inequality. On the contrary recent research points in the opposite direction. If we want to help some of the most disadvantages groups in society, then encouraging deeper private sector involvements is likely to be the best way forward.

Several developments are underway in India, all of which involve the private education sector meeting the needs of the poor in distinct ways. But India is not unique in this respect—similar phenomena are happening all over the developing world.

As a point of departure, how do government schools serve the poor? Usefully, the government sponsored Public Report on Basic Education in India (PROBE) from 1999 paints a very bleak picture of the "malfunctioning" of government schools for the poor. When researchers called unannounced on their random sample of schools, only 53 per cent had any "teaching activity' going on. In 33 percent, the head teacher was absent. Alarmingly, the team noted that the deterioration of teaching standards was not to do with disempowered teachers, but instead could be ascribed to "plain negligence." They noted "several cases of irresponsible teachers keeping a school closed....for months at a time," many cases of drunk teachers, and head teachers who asked children to do domestic chores. Significantly, the low level of teaching activity occurred even in those schools with relative good infrastructure, teaching aids and pupil-teacher ratios.

But is there any alternative to these schools? Surely no-one else can do better than government given the resources available? As it happens, the PROBE report were serving the poor and conceded—rather reluctantly—such problems were not found in these schools. In the great majority of private schools—again visited unannounced and at random—there" was feverish classroom activity." Most parents would prefer to send their children to private schools if they could afford them. Private schools, they said, were successful because they were more accountable: "the teachers are accountable to the manager (who can fire them), and, through him or her, to the parents (who can withdraw their children)." Such accountability was not present in the government schools, and "this contrast is perceived with crystal clarity by the vast majority of parents".

The Way Forward: Loosen Regulations and Set up Voucher Schemes

To many readers, the existence of these private schools for the poor will come as a surprise. It was to me too, until I had the privilege of conducting field work for the International Finance Corporation (the private finance arm of the World Bank) on a group of such schools operating under the banner of the Federation of Private Schools" management based in Hyderabad, the federation has 500 private schools (from kindergarten to grade ten) serving poor communities in slums and villages. I was impressed by both the entrepreneurial spirit within these schools—they were run on commercial principles, not dependent on hand-outs from state or philanthropy—but also by the spirit of dedication within the schools for the poor communities served: not for nothing were the leaders of the schools known as "social workers". But these schools suffer under restrictive and inappropriate regulations. One example will suffice: to be recognised a school must deposit upto 50,000 rupees (about $1.200) in a stipulated bank account, of which neither the capital nor the interest can be touched. Given that the fees charged in these schools ranged from 25 (60 cents) to Rs. 150 per month (about $3.50) with most of the schools grouped near the lower end of the range, such sums are completely prohibitive.

Fees of around $10 per year are not affordable by everyone, but they are to a large number of poor families. Furthermore, the great majority of the schools offer a significant number of free places—up to 20 per cent—for the poorest students, allocated on the basis of claims of need checked informally in the community.

All of this suggests that if one is interested in serving the needs of the poor in India, then trying to reform the totally inadequate, cumbersome and unaccountable government system is unlikely to be the best way. Instead, reform the regulatory environment to make it suitable for the flourishing of private schools for the poor, help build private financing schemes using overseas and indigenous philanthropy, and encourage public voucher schemes so that parents can use their allowance of funding where they see the schools are performing well, rather than wasting them in unresponsive state schools.

Private education in developing countries isn't just about the poor, of course, and there are many exciting examples of big education businesses. But these too have implications for the ways in which the private sector can reach the least advantaged. One Indian company which embodies much of the excite the National Institute for Information Technology (NIIT). With its competitor, Aptech, it shares just over 70 per cent of the information technology education and training market in India estimated at roughly Rs. 1.1 billion ($24 million). NIIT has 40 wholly owned centres in the metropolitan areas, and about 1,000 franchised centres across India. It also has a global reach, with centres in the U.S. Asian Pacific, Europe, Japan, Central Asia and Africa. A key aspect of NIIT's educational philosophy is that there is a need to harness research to improve the efficiency of learning and to raise educational standards.

Because of its success in developing innovative and cost-effective IT education and training, NIIT has attracted the attention to several state governments. First off the mark was Tamil Nadu, which wanted to bring a computer curriculum to all of its high schools. Significantly, although allocating about $22 million over five years to this endeavour, it didn't hand the funds over to government schools, perhaps in light of the PROBE report's lessons. Instead, it developed a model to contract out the service to private companies, which provide the software and hardware, while the government supplies electricity and the class room. For the first round of the Tamil Nadu process, 43 contracts were awarded for 666 schools, with NIIT allotted 371 schools. Many of the classrooms have become NIIT centre, open to school children and teachers I daytime, then used by the franchise holder in the evenings. The contracting out of curriculum areas such as this represents an important step forward in relationships between the public and private sectors, and provides an interesting model worth watching and emulating.

Most recently, NIIT has focused on reaching largely illiterate and unschooled children through the Internet. Within weeks of having set up an "Internet kiosk" in a slum area, the institute's researchers found that without any instruction, children could achieve a remarkable level of computer literacy. NIIT is exploring ways to roll out the idea commercially, harnessing the power of the private sector to reach the poorest through modern technology.

These initiatives all find echoes in other developing countries. In each case, the private, not the public sector, is most responsive to the needs of the poor, and is brining innovation, efficiency and educational quality to the lives of the most disadvantaged. The private sector has the potential to promote greater equity and to influence education policy, provided it is encouraged and viewed as a partner, not a threat to governments, whether in the developing or the developed world.

5

For a Broader Approach to Education

In our rapidly changing world, literacy should be seen as an important evolutionary variable in every society. For the further a society progresses, the more it needs to adjust and adapt to new demands and pressures, so that literacy is lifelong necessity for all.

Literacy, in the broad sense, is the foundation for life skills, ranging from basic oral and written communication to the ability to solve scientific and social problems. Today it involves much more than the acquisition of 3 Rs. And a limited set of traditional skills. It is linked with the changing demands of life in a given socio-cultural context.

This means that local communities should be fully involved in defining the content of literacy programmes. The local dimension of literacy is externally important, not only for accommodating the real needs of learners, but also for taking into account the linguistic and cultural realities of multicultural societies. For in the end, only the learners actually decide what they need to learn.

Building Bridges Between Cultures

Most literacy specialist have a accepted this broader, more dynamic and culturally sensitive stance. It marks a long overdue acknowledgement of the positive role that local language and cultures can play in removing some of the serious pedagogical and psychological hurdles often encountered by learners, it is the only way to ensure the relevance and authority of literacy work.

Any one can insist here on the importance of multilingual education. Today education is as much about learning to live together as learning to know, to do and to be. Yet we cannot live together if our possibilities of expression are limited to a single linguistic frame. This is often at the root of problems encountered in multicultural societies. Of course, inequality in all its forms is a major factor. But internal conflicts often have purely cultural causes. It is more difficult for people to forge links with each other when they cannot communicate linguistically.

Yet children learn languages easily—much more so than the adults who take the decisions. We need to take much greater advantage of this fact. Children are expected to store too much information in their "hard memory"—much of it frankly useless! Giving them language skills provides them with bridges between cultures, enabling them to grow up without the debilitating sense that other cultures are lien. It is our task to try to ensure that education at all levels, and particularly basic education, promotes multilinguism. And we must invest in such education, since to do so is to invest in peace.

It is also important to remind ourselves that literacy is not a neutral process which can be applied in all situations, all the time, regardless of social and economic realities. Such a narrow concept of literacy ignores its critical role as a tool of empowerment. One can treat adult learners as empty vessels waiting to be filled with predetermined bodies of knowledge disconnected from their social experience. Literacy must provide space of intellectual development, motivations for learning and a sense of self-esteem, if it is to be a genuine education for empowerment.

Bringing Adult Education into the Mainstream

Many individuals and families around the world are facing unexpected changes in the pattern of their daily lives, disrupting their plans for the future. The demands on educational services are increasing dramatically, especially in countries where the state is the main provider of education for children and adults. In today's world, we cannot afford a short-sighted approach which, in effect, excludes adult education from the mainstream of the education system, even after the concept of life long learning has been accepted as a framework for educational policy.

Literacy programmes must be given the priority they deserve. Lifelong learning for all requires quality adult education and literacy programmes with qualified personnel, relevant teaching programmes, appropriate post-literacy materials and decent facilities. We must ask ourselves whether we recently are prepared to make the necessary; investments in adult education and literacy to ensure universal access to the types of programmes needed to reach the targets of education for all.

If we truly believe in lifelong learning, and if we seriously believe in redressing the balance of learning in our societies, then we should seek to develop in every country an open and more enabling system of education, breaking with past concepts of education as something which happens to people between the ages of six and twenty and which only the privileged of few were entitled to. Synergy has to be created between formal and non-formal education programmes.

A case in point is the family literacy concept. We all know that the continuing education of parents, particularly when they are illiterate or under-educated, can contribute very effectively to their children's success in school. In fact the family literacy approach is one of the must effective ways of breaking the cycle of inter-generational illiteracy. Education and training policies should include all types of learning, whether it takes place in a school, in the workplace or at home. There should be more innovation and creativity in using methods and approaches.

6

Wiring up the Ivory Towers

Prestigious universities are forging alliances to conquer a share of the e-learning market and stand up to virtual competitors. Just like airline companies, universities around the world are forming partnerships and consortia in response to the pressures of globalization. The World Education Market held in Vancouver was a timely sign: the fair, expressly organised to foster relations between universities, training providers, software companies and representatives from nations with large education needs attracted participants from over 60 countries.

This race to "partner up" is fuelled by a number of factors. In most industrialised countries, government funding for higher education has decreased, forcing institutions to look for new markets either to subsidize campus programmes or just to remain viable. There is a growing need for lifelong learning as "jobs for life" vanish and the information society drastically reduces the shelf-life of almost any educational qualification. Technological developments, increasingly necessary for learners in all fields to master, offer ever more innovative tools for supporting e-learning.

For business, online learning is "the" new market opportunity with the need for re-training and professional updating predicted to crease an $11.5 billion industry by 2003. Business is better able to develop and maintain the technological infrastructure necessary to run large online systems and everyone, including the universities, recognizes that it takes robust telecommunications technology to deliver education and training on the scale demanded.

A host of companies has sprung up to help universities shape and package courses for online presentation, while network providers are jockeying for position to deliver online education.

The United States is the undisputed leader in the field, prompting governments in the U.K., Canada and Australia to commission being eroded by U.S. ventures turned global Canada and the U.K. are in the early stages of setting up their own virtual universities. But what has become clear is that the conservative and labyrinthine decision-making processes which characterize most university procedures are being jolted by a race to get a share of the lifelong learning market.

So far, the most common approach for universities to break into the e-learning universe has been to develop courses specifically for a corporate partner or to form alliances among themselves. Universities 21, a company incorporated in the U.K. is a network of 18 leading universities in ten countries.

Very often, prestigious universities has stayed clear of going fully online, seeing a danger to their brand name. Many are limiting their offerings to continuing education programmes and/or non-degree courses, and more often than not, they are aiming at the corporate market. One Company Unext. com, has partnered with first-class institutions such as the University of Columbia (U.S.) and the London School of Economics to create online courses marketed under the name Cardean University. Their target: the Fortune 500 companies as well as individual adults. They've managed to attract noble laureates to design courses and the universities have formed spin-off for-profit companies specifically to develop online programmes. This facilities the commercialisation of software and other products, and is a way to take a commercial approach to continuing and professional studies without compromising the Univesity's standing.

Then there are the free-standing for profit virtual universities which are arousing the ire of institutions that have prided themselves on a long history of public service. The most quoted examplar is Phonenix University, the largest private outfit in the U.S. Now owned by the Apollo Group, it operates the country's largest online programme with 12,200 students. The university tracks students progress and contacts those who don't submit assignments on time or fail to enrol in subsequent courses. Many critics question Phonenix's blatant commercialization, but few doubt the university's impact on continuing professional development provision.

Although e-learning is in its infancy, its impact can already by gauged. New providers are coming on the market all the time and the trend is accelerating to the point of upsetting universities virtual monopoly in educational accreditation. An Information Technology training course offered or accredited by Microsoft has undoubtedly become more valuable than a Bachelor of Science from a renowned university.

The more consumerist the approach of the education provider, the more what is taught is influenced by demand. MBAs dominate e-learning provision and IT courses are a close second. While the new consumer/learner demands flexibility, choice and just-in-time learning opportunities, suppliers will inevitably arise who are focused on meeting the demand at the expense of quality and value. And is the consumer really the best judge of what course material to choose? Education is a more complex "product" than toothpaste or washing powder. A totally consumer driven education market is unlikely to be in society's best interest in the long term. The commercialisation of education usually goes hand-in-hand with desegregation: course design, delivery, tutoring assessment and accreditation may be carried out by different organisations. Students might study courses or modules from different universities or providers and then put themselves forward for examination and accreditation by yet another institution. While most academics loathe marking assignments, they regard this scenario with horror, and blame commercialisation for the demise of the 'community of scholars' concept of a university. The death of the 'course' has also been predicted, with learners—especially corporate and on-the job learners—demanding short study modules. What then happens to the ability to get an overview of a field when learning consists of the students selecting a whole series of unconnected learning "bites"? Learners will be "zapping" between short sequences or presentations much as they do between television channels.

But while some faculty view e-learning with alarm, technology-based learning is where most of the pedagogical innovation is taking place in universities. Multimedia learning resources and interactive simulations are being developed for the web. Collaborative learning activities, new forms of online assessment and small group teaching technologies are making online courses more stimulating, interactive and attractive than many face-to-face taught courses.

Despite "doom and gloom scenarios", most moderate observers of the scene see a continued future for the campus university, especially at the undergraduate level, while e-learning will above all cater to adult professional and independent learners. Some commercialisation of education is good if it fosters innovation, concern for quality and responsiveness to consumer demands. But if some is good, more is not necessarily better! Not in education at least.

7

Population Growth and Education

In contrast to the food supply challenge posed by the coming wave of population growth, the global need for teachers and classrooms will rise very slowly in the next half-century. In many countries, the school-age population is increasing much less rapidly than the overall national population. The trend illustrates that growth rates typically differ for different age strata of the population. It has also shows that declining birth rates can take decades to move through an entire population.

At the global level, for example, total population is projected to increase by 54 per cent between 2000 and 2050, but the number of children aged 5 to 14 will grow by only 6 per cent. And of the world's largest countries-accounting for 60 per cent of global population in 1995—will actually begin to see decreases in the number of children aged 5 to 14 by 2015; for several of these countries, the decline in this age group has already begun. These countries will need fewer classrooms and teachers to educate the youngest members of society (assuming they maintain current class size and student-teacher ratios).

Planetary of nations, however, still have increasingly child-age populations. Where countries have not acted to stabilize population, the base of the national population pyramid continues to expand, and pressures on the educational system will be severe. In the world's 10 fastest-growing countries, for example, most of which are in Africa and the Middle East, the child-age population will increase in average 93 per cent over the next half-century. Africa as a whole will see its school-age population grow by 75 per cent through 2040.

Many countries will be challenged to increase funding for education while ensuring that other worthy sectors also receive the support they need. With 900 million illiterate adults in the world, the case for a renewed commitment to education is easy to make. But competing for these funds are the 840 million chronically hungry and the 1.2 billion without access to a decent toilet.

The budget stresses on governments attempting to meet these basic needs would clearly be reduced with smaller populations. Mozambique and Lesotho, for example, both met the UNESCO benchmark for investment in education in 1992—6 per cent of gross domestic product-and the two countries economies were roughly equal in size. Yet because Mozambique has many times the population of Lesotho, spending per child in Lesotho is about nine times higher than in Mozambique. For the majority of countries who do not meet the UNESCO funding standard, many of whom also fall short in providing other basic services, a decline in population pressure could help substantially to meet all of their social goals.

If national education systems begin to stress life-long learning for a rapidly changing world, as recommended by a 1998 UNESCO report on education in the twenty-first century, then extensive provision for adult education will be necessary, affecting even those countries with shrinking childgage populations, such a development means that countries that started population stabilisation programmes earliest will be in the best position to educate their entire citizenry.

8

Violence in Schools: *A World Wide Affair*

In all countries, schools are magnets for strife in society. Dealing with these tensions calls for extreme caution, for fear of making matters worse. Violence in schools is a world wide problem; it exists in rich and poor countries alike. It's chiefly a male phenomenon, hitting a peak when boys turn 16 years old in some countries and 13 in others. Experts agree at least on one point: this violence cannot be pinned to a single cause. Instead, they point to complex patterns linked to family situations. Socio-economic conditions and teaching methods.

Tackling Segregation

But these are just indicators and do not justify any deterministic explanations. When researchers say that 10 to 20 per cent of risk factors are linked to single parent families, this suggests that 80 to 90 per cent of such families are not the source of any violence. A child form a slum area with a teenage mother or a father in jail will not automatically be violent! Likewise, experts say there is a "hard core" of violent children—about five per cent of the total. One can found that this figure can vary between one and 11 per cent. The school itself can be an aggravating factor, through high staff turnover or "ghetto classes" to which poorly-performing studies are relegated. These "hard core" groups, then, cannot be deemed "inalterable". On the contrary, something can be done about them.

Should they simply be expelled, as some advocate? Such a measure would only make their segregation and sense of exclusion worse. And they are, after all, at the root of the whole problem. The solution lies partly in developing customised projects, but most importantly, in strengthening economic social participation.

To put an end to school violence, we need a well-established state with the means to compensate for inequalities, a state that tries to re-establish diversity in neighbourhoods and schools, one that does not give up on the notion of justice for children, as some are demanding.

Passing the Torch

We should also try to lift schools out of their fortresses, so they do not become the symbol of a society that excludes people. Projects in the Netherlands, Brazil and the United States have shown that schools can be vibrant places that provide social medical and cultural services to a neighbourhood.

In the Brazilian state of Minas Gerais, for example, there is a vocational school where elderly craftsmen teach their skills to teenagers. Such contact between generations can offer a very valuable social education. "It takes a village to educate a child", goes an effort an African proverb. Let's make an effort to seek out these opportunities, even in the most heartless cities.

9

Helping Your Child Learn

A one-syllable word begins the education process: "Why?" Parents are always trying to answer that question. And that interaction between parent and child is the basis of much that children learn.

Teaching and learning are not mysteries that can happen only in school. They can also happen when parents and children do simple things together—things such as:

- Figure out whose socks are whose-sorting is a major function in maths and science.
- Cook a meal to learn science and good health.
- Tell each other a story as an important beginning for reading and writing; if the story is about the past, it's a way to interest a child in history.
- Plan a visit to a friend or relative for a personal connection with geography.
- Or play a game of hopscotch to develop counting and lifelong fitness.
- All children love their friends. So ask your child to describe his friend's appearance at the end of each school day. You can ask questions like. "What outfit did he/she wear?" or "How did he/she do his/her hair? This kind of routine query would encourage your child to observe his friend more minutely.
- If your child goes to school by bus, he can be asked to describe his route and point out certain landmarks

namely colourful posters, traffic signals, large shops etc.

By doing things with their children, parents show that learning is fun and important—and that encourages children to study, learn, and stay in school.

Even on the discipline front, parents can help their children. Basic disciplinary principles must be tailored to each child and family. Before parents can become effective disciplinarians, they must first learn how to manage their own anger, solve problem situations and give and get support from others. Simple self-help techniques with or without professional support can help parents sharply reduce discipline problems.

Parents who are sensitive to their children's needs have more obedient children. Praise and love alone are not enough to instil good behaviour. Too much permissiveness hurts a child's efforts to develop self-control.

Behaviour problems should be reversed early. Waiting until the preteen-age years diminishes chances for success and puts children at higher risk for drug use and other problems.

Parents need to learn as many tricks of the trade as possible, including how to play with their children, communicate with them, praise and reward them and also set limits for them, as well as how to handle misbehaviour using a variety of techniques.

All that parents need to help their children is a willingness to observe and learn with them, and, to take the time to nurture their natural curiosity.

10

Beyond Economics

Unless policymakers take a more all-round view of education, they risk sending their countries down the wrong path. Over the past decade, educational change in most countries has been driven by one imperative: survival in the global economy. This process has been particularly salient in the Asia-Pacific region following the drastic shock of the 1997 economic downturn. But in the current reform process, marked by speeding commercialisation and economic preoccupations, other educational missions are being ignored, and countries risk paying a high price for their short-sightedness.

There's no denying that economic considerations are critical in today's world. Students have to acquire the knowledge and skills to survive and compete in the global economy, especially one which more than ever before prizes human capital. A high-quality labour force gives nations a cutting edge in global competition. Understandably, stressing economic returns in the current educational debate attracts private resources. But education has other functions that are the indispensable corollary of more balanced, equitable development. They deserve to be briefly explained.

The first is a social function: education has a role to play in facilitating social mobility and bringing about integration in often very diverse constituencies. It is at school that children learn how to form a broader set of relationships, to live together and become aware of belonging to teach us civic attitudes, to make us aware of our rights and responsibilities—in essence, to become responsible citizens. The task is fundamental in light of democracy's advance in so many countries over the past decade or so. Then there is education's cultural function. Developing creativity and aesthetic awareness, accepting other traditions and belief systems while valuing our own are all part of the path towards fulfilment. Finally, education is a goal in and of itself. Schools help children learn how to learn and play a pivotal role in transferring knowledge from one generation to the next. I believe that all these facets of learning are critical for the long-term prosperity of our societies. In our globalised, interdependent world, these functions take on a more international character. Everywhere, education has a role to play in eliminating racial and gender biases, promoting global common interests, moments for peace, and greater international understanding.

Rising Above Short-term Pressures to Strike a Harmonious Balance

While education is widely recognised as the spine of the learning society, the complexity lies in striking a balance between these various functions. The commercialisation of education that we are witnessing the world over inevitably pushes schools, educators, parents and policymakers to pursue short-term, market-driven outcomes. Lawyers, bankers and businessmen have an increasingly high profile in educational debates. Following Southeast Asia's downturn in 1997, they were influential in changing the academic mindset. In little time, emphasis has shifted from academic achievement to developing communication skills, creativity, adaptability. In and of itself this is not necessarily regrettable. The problem is that these skills are all perceived to be at the service of a supreme economic value.

Sounder research will be required to analyse and assess where the current trends are leading us. It is increasingly recognised however, that unless economic growth is accompanied by good governance, a fair sharing of benefits, better social and environmental protection and attention to culture, it will, sooner or later, lead to unrest. It is through education that this broad spectrum of concerns can be nurtured. Policymakers who have taken stock of this holistic mission unfortunately represent a minority in today's educational debates and reforms. Their foremost challenge is to manage commercialization, to rise above short-term pressures and to take a more ethical stance towards education, a long-term strategic view.

11

Population Growth and Jobs

Since mid-century, the world's labour force has more than doubled-from 1.2 billion people to 2.7 billion, outstripping the growth in job creation. As a result, the United Nations International Labour Organisation estimates that nearly 1 billion people, approximately 30 per cent of the global work force, are unemployed or underemployed (working but not earning enough to meet basic needs). Over the next half—century, the world will need to create more than 1.9 billion jobs-all of them in the developing world—just to maintain current levels of employment.

As economists often note, while population growth may boost labour demand (through economic activity and demand for goods), it will most definitely boost labour supply. During the next 50 years, almost 40 million people will enter the global labour force—defined as those between the ages of 15 and 65 seeking work-each year. Between 1995 and 2050, some 1.9 billion additional jobs will need to be created to absorb these new would-be workers. The most pressing needs will be found in the world's poorest nations—a sobering example of the vicious cycle linking poverty and population growth.

As the children of today represent the workers of tomorrow, the interaction between population growth and jobs is most acute in nations with young populations. Nations such as Peru, Mexico, Indonesia, and Zambia with more than half their population below the age of 25 will feel the burden of this labour flood. In the Middle East and Africa, 40 per cent of the population is under the age of 15. Since new entrants into the labour force were born at least 15 years ago, measures to reduce population growth have a delayed effect on the growth of the labour force, highlighting the urgency of taking action on population.

Nowhere is the employment challenge greater than in Africa, where at least 40 per cent of the population lives in absolute poverty. Although 8 million people entered the sub-Saharan work force in 1997, by 2030 this resource-scarce region will have to absorb more than 17 million new entrants each year. Over the next half-century, Nigeria's labour force is projected to grow by 246 per cent and Ethiopia's will soar by 337 per cent—both faster than growth of the general population. At current growth rates, the size of the labour force in sub-Saharan Africa will more than triple by 2050.

As a result of unprecedented population growth and increasing acceptance of female participation in the work force, the number of people seeking jobs in the Middle East and North Africa, a region already plagued by double-digit unemployment rates, will double in the next 50 years. In Algeria, where unemployment stands at 22 per cent, the labour force is growing at a staggering 4.2 per cent annually, and the number seeking work will more than double by 2050. Egypt alone will need to create 26 million more jobs by 2050 as its total population hits 115 million.

Nations throughout Asia will also see phenomenal increases in the numbers seeking work, including Pakistan, where the work force will grow from 70 million in 1998 to 205 million by 2050. Over the next 25 years, India will add nearly 10 million to its work force each year. During the same period, China will add nearly 6 million annually due to population growth alone, compounding the work shortages caused by the current flood of migrants to China's coastal cities and by massive layoffs—estimated at more than 30 million—as state-run operations are scaled back.

Nations are hard-pressed to educate and train rapidly growing numbers of young people in marketable skills for the global workplace. Moreover, meeting the basic needs of a growing population draws scarce foreign exchange and other resources from investments in education and job creation. Throughout the world, young people entering the work force are increasingly faced with unemployment and social marginalisation. In most societies, unemployment rates for those under 25 are substantially higher than for older people.

Surplus farmland once served as a traditional source of employment for growing populations, as new land could be ploughed to generate work and income. However, global percapita Greenland has dropped by half and considerably more in certain nations since 1950. Moreover, the machanisation of agriculture fuels the exodus of job seekers into the world's urban areas, where unemployment is often most acute heavily reliant on natural capital in the past, future job creation will require massive amounts of financial capital to jump-start the industrial and service sectors.

As the balance between the demand and supply of labour is tipped by population growth, wages—the price of labour-tend to decrease. And in a situation of labour surplus, the quality of jobs may not improve as fast for workers will settle for longer hours, fewer benefits and less control over work activities.

Employment is the key to obtaining food, housing, health services, and education, in addition to providing self-respect and self-fulfilment. Rising numbers of unemployed people could drive global poverty and hunger to precarious levels, fueling political instability.

12

Employment and Poverty Alleviation

Today the key socio-economic problem is large-scale unemployment. Spreading joblessness brings many other problems in its wake. It erodes national income and living standards, aggravating the already grindingly difficult job of promoting development and alleviating poverty. Joblessness also raises government budget deficits, increasing macro-economic instability while soaking up investment for productive capital expenditure, education, training and relief aid. And joblessness ruins lives and communities by depriving people of the dignity and satisfaction that comes with earning one's keep and making a contribution to the well being of family and society.

Theories about how best to nurture development (and thus create jobs) have shifted considerably over the last decade. The state role has evolved, in the minds of many, from being a source of relief for the problems of unemployment, poverty and underdevelopment, to being a fundamental cause of these problems through the distorting impact of its intervention on the market.

However, the more market oriented philosophy that grew up during the 1990s has yet to provide convincing solutions in practice at least not on a grand scale and especially not in terms of job creation as the present jobless economic recovery demonstrates.

The weakness of the current recovery and past approaches to economic development can be traced to the failure to consider employment as the predominant means of promoting growth and alleviating poverty. In policy circles it has too long been an almost ignored priority.

Current trends thus bode poorly, particularly as unemployment rates soar. In light of the circumstances, we need to begin re-examining some of the fundamental questions—if only to find out what has gone wrong with the answers.

Minimum Wage?

Let's begin with wages. With corporate restructuring in full force on a global scale, are low wage rates required to raise employment and maximize profits? A top manager of a multinational consumer electronics group certainly thinks so; he likened the perfect factory to a ship "so that we could move it around the world to where labour was cheapest". Perhaps, but this bottom-line emphasis on unit labour costs ignores at least two other factors; namely, that higher wages can act as a screen to select more productive workers and that higher wages translate into better productivity via improved worker nutrition, increased consumption and a generally healthier quality of life.

If higher wages bring these benefits (and it is an open question) should government insist that there be a minimum wage rate? Neo-classical economists tend to respond "no", assuming that a higher wage rate puts money into the pockets of some low wage workers while forcing many others out of work because companies cannot afford to pay them.

Technology Transfer

The impact of technology is another area in need of study. Technological innovation is usually labour-saving and tends to originate in industrialised countries, moving toward developing countries like India, Pakistan where labour tends to be low cost and abundant. Would it therefore make sense to slow down or somehow restrict technology transfer, especially to development markets, in the interest of preserving employment?

The answer here is clearly—no. Historical evidence abundantly demonstrates that attempts to retard technological progress bring about grater poverty and lower growth. Technology, infact, is at the heart of the new endogenous growth theory which is very much in vogue among development economists today. Slowing down or inhibiting technology transfer would certainly dash many countries' development hopes and aggravate poverty. However, the relationship between technology, development, employment and poverty alleviation is not without its complications.

In the 1980s, the buzz word among development specialists was "appropriate technology", i.e., small-scale and labour-intensive technologies that would increase productive output while allowing an equilibrium solution to be found such that the ratio of the productivity of labour to that of capital is proportional to their relative prices. The conditions for this "small is beautiful" approach to technology tended to be best met in agricultural production. However, where manufacturing industry is concerned, the small-is-beautiful approach foundered badly when the only viable technological alternatives proved to be highly capital-intensive.

Development Gap

A wide gap has emerged between developing countries with an inward focus (which tended to be projectionist and pursue policies of import substitution) and those with an outward focus and a policy of pursuing export-led growth. Competing in international markets requires technology that is as good as or better than that found in advanced, industrialised nations. Small, therefore, is not beautiful in the global manufacturing economy where product standards are high and the elasticity of substitution between labour and capital is very limited.

The drive to obtain state-of-the-art technology thus leads to a policy conundrum: it is a pre-condition for success in manufactured exports, but the impulse to compete successfully in this most lucrative sector speeds up the transfer of technology from the developed to the developing world, thus reinforcing the bias toward labour saving equipment in developing countries and accelerating a process that is seen as a source of job loss in the industrialised countries.

Technology and Jobs

Before concluding that modern technology transfer is inimical to employment in developing countries, we have to distinguish clearly between technology's static and dynamic consequences. In a static sense, it is true that highly capital-intensive export industries may not create much employment on a net basis, but the dynamic effects of technology transfer do contribute to economic growth. And growth, in turn, generates multiplier effects in the form of demand, which stimulates ancillary production activities (like food processing or consumer goods) that rely on more labour-intensive technologies.

The problem is that the diffusion and application of technology on a global scale blurs the categories of international product specialisation and creates a much more competitive and conflict-prone international environment.

For example, we have already seen the Asian Tigers move from producing goods such as textiles and processed food to producing hi-tech and value-added consumer durables. This advance is only possible due to the growth of human capital (facilitated by investment and higher incomes) and it leaves production of textiles to other industrializing countries, like Indonesia, the Philippines and now China. But the dynamic comes at the expense of jobs in industrialised regions, like the US and the EC, which lost more than a quarter of their work force in textiles during the 1980s. Inspite of job losses, advanced countries continue to produce textiles, notwithstanding major differences in the hourly wage rates for spinning and weaving and the fact that essentially the same hi tech equipment is being used in most production centres.

Protectionism

What has happened in textiles is happening in other industrial sectors (automobiles, for example) as well. The intense market competition is providing to be a source of trade conflicts, and possibly protectionism, as jobs come under increasing pressure.

For many workers and managers, the benefits of foreign direct investment look increasingly like a zero-sum game for employment, and there is a real risk that the tenuous link between overall growth and employment will break down altogether. It is hardly surprising that we are already seeing negatively affected workers and local businesses clamouring for protection in advanced countries.

Governments Role

The concerned governments are suppose to carry out much of this research. The three initial lines of inquiry follow from three reasonable assumptions about the future.

- First, increase in welfare and consumption subsidies are out; investments in training and human capital are in. How can investments in human capital be directed to positive employment effects? Is it perhaps not time to explore more fully benefit schemes targeting the unemployed and the unskilled poor providing them with the type of subsidies that would enhance their human capital, improve their health and productivity through better nutrition and preventive medicine, and restore the dignity of holding a job?
- Second, given the quasi-inevitability of increased automation in manufacturing, how can other sectors (particularly agriculture and services) be developed to export their long-term potential for employment creation?
- Third, given the inevitable pressures of work and productivity in the global economy, what sort. of alternative institutional arrangements need to evolve with respect to industrial relations, employment and work conditions?

Finding answers to these and other questions will require no small amount of new thinking, but parochialism or a failure of imagination would be fatal flaws in this global era.

13

Solving the Unemployment Problem by Looking Beyond the Job

If you had a job, you worked; if you didn't, you didn't. Having a job meant being employed by an organisation in a clearly-defined and stable occupational role, with duties, hours, rates of pay and promotion all more or less standardised. But the job-in that meaning of the world—is a social invention, and a fairly recent one.

The job—the kind that you had, or hoped to get-because a central fixture of life. Its importance was great because it served many needs: For managers and efficiency experts, job assignments were the key to assembly-line manufacturing. For union organizers, jobs protected the rights of workers. For political reformers, standardised civil service positions were the essence of good government. Jobs provided an identify the immigrants and recently-urbanised farm workers. They provided a sense of security for individuals and an organising principle for society.

Jobs functioned in so many ways that it is surprising how many organizations are now opting for other ways to define and manage work. The second job shift is underway. Its emergence can be seen in the increasing use of temporary and part-time workers and contracted-out services, the changing relationships between workers and management, the growing popularity of self-employment and small business. Indeed, "de-jobbing" is proceeding at such a pace that many economists, management experts and futurists are now taking freely about the end of the job. Bridges predicts that the job as we now know it will disappear entirely—replaced by new kinds of flexible work assignments in post-job organizations—and be remembered only as a quaint artefact of the industrial age.

One reason for the change in work is the economic rules of the survival game among organizations that employ workers. To stay successful in today's hitech consumer economy, business have had to re-model themselves into what some experts call "agile companies"—ones that are able to respond quickly to conditions in ever-changing, fragmenting, competitive markets.

The "knowledge worker", whose work involves not simply doing something, but also applying theoretical or analytical skills. Such workers are replacing the industrial labourer as the dominant part of the workforce—and their productive activities are likely to be organised and structured much differently from those of their assembly-line predecessors.

De-jobbing as a result of new technology or the emergence of a service economy is a phenomenon that gets a lot of attention these days; but it is not the whole story. At all levels of society, people are improvising livelihoods that do not fit the industrial-era model. Immigrants to the developed countries, often unable to find steady jobs, nevertheless find places in the new landscape by being mobile, flexible, resourceful and imaginative: they moonlight, work part-time, share jobs, start small businesses. Their lives are often extremely difficult, but they are also instructive to those of us who believe you either have a job or you're out of luck.

It is too early to evaluate the implications of this multifaceted transformation of work, or to dismiss it as simply good or bad. Nevertheless, one cannot deny that it is taking place, and will bring about dramatic social changes.

On the downside, the job shift is causing great hardships for many workers and their families. It posses serious challenges to policy-makers, political activists and labour leaders. The basic question appears to be whether the key to global employment-development strategy is to play "catch-up"—trying to bring millions of people around the world into jobs in industries and the public sector, or to play "leapfrog" crating new forms of employment.

The proposal to generate more employment in agriculture, for example, is based on new demand for agricultural exports from developing countries. The policies designed to make the most of this opportunity include measures to upgrade technology, raise productivity, ensure the supply of essential inputs, establish marketing and distribution channels, create links between agriculture and industry, and cater to export markets.

The issue of part-time work, another kind of employment that is seriously undervalued in the traditional industrial era job mind-set. Part time work may not offer much at this point to developing countries, where many people are under employed and wages are low, but it can be of great help in more advanced economies. And it is likely to be a big part of the global work picture in the years ahead.

A certain agility may also be necessary in agriculture, particularly in countries that for many years have depended heavily on producing commodities such as sugar for export as a means of generating income and employment. As Northern laboratories develop non-agricultural substitutes for many of these commodities—and this is already beginning to happen—the bottom may fall out of "monoculture" economies, only economic, but will have long-run political implications as communities attempt to recognize themselves in response to the changed conditions. It is, therefore, in the interest of raw materials exporters to closely monitor current trends in biotechnology and the use of genetic resources and modify their internal policies in anticipation of potential long-term effects."

This calls for flexibility, and an ability to get information and to act on it. Government officials, development workers, community leaders and individuals will, in some respects, all have to be "knowledge workers" if they are to keep ahead of global changes. Jobs are going to be crated not just by putting people to work, but by finding—or creating-new niches where they can be productive.

It is still possible to talk about jobs for all, and to resist the assumption made by many economists that high levels of unemployment are now inevitable. But, as we move ahead into the global information economy, we may be moving back into an older conception of the job, and seeing it again as something you do, rather than as something you have—or that has you.

14

Technological Entrepreneurship: *The New Force for Economic Growth*

Entrepreneurship has emerged as a major new force for change. The dynamic role of modern small business in economic growth has received fresh recognition worldwide. It is essential to promote entrepreneurship and to mobilize the dynamism of the private sector for accelerated national development. An unbridled private sector may not, however, ensure growth with equity. It is the prime responsibility of governments to create policy frameworks that enable business to apply technology for competitive advantage and for the well-being of the public.

The Changing Global Environment

As agents of change and progress, entrepreneurs start by identifying a market opportunity and matching this with social or technical innovations. They then proceed to mobilize the resources necessary to drive their business concept to its commercial realization. The development of a product or service with a high-technology content—never easy anywhere, or at today's rapidly-changing global environment. It calls for restructuring the available technology and business development systems and developing the skills needed by a new breed of "techno-entrepreneurs" to transform innovations into market opportunities at home and abroad. It also requires reorienting the present processes and priorities of technical and economic cooperation among countries.

Amidst the global concerns of environmental preservation, poverty elimination and social development, the practical problems of entrepreneurship are not being properly addressed, even though entrepreneurs will create the bulk of enterprises, jobs and wealth.

A torrent of technology-based goods hits the market every week, ostensibly improving the quality of our lives while simultaneously creating complexity and dislocation. The pace of progress in information technologies, microelectronics, robotics, new materials, biomedical sciences, space science and other advanced technologies quickens, significantly changing the way we live. The growth of markets for these technologies also proceeds apace.

Further, technological change is taking place today against a background of growing intra-national and international disequilibria. While the transformation from State-centred to market-oriented development is opening up enormous opportunities and options, it has also caused severe short-term hardships. In order to survive and prosper in these changing times, India and its enterprises need enlightened government policies, good technical infrastructure and strong cultural roots.

Traditional production factors are giving way to a new paradigm characterised by new patterns of trade, investment and employment, and by informal networking life-long learning and technological entrepreneurship. The manufacturing sector in India continues to be dominated by food products, textiles, chemicals and other traditional industry, mainly in the public sector. However, change is coming, albeit slowly. State enterprises are being corporatised pending privatization, and the share of knowledge-based and information-related activities in the marketplace is rising perceptibly. Restructuring policies now place emphasis (often purely rhetorical) on the role of the private sector. The legacy of decades of centrally-planned development is generally inimical to private enterprise. In turn, the private sector has been slow to respond to economic liberalisation in India and generally failed to generate the new employment necessary to absorb new entrants to the labour force.

The regulatory problems of an onerous tax structure and administration, poor access to finance and raw materials, over-regulation of labour and land use, pervasive bureaucracy and restricted markets have been significant barriers to entrepreneurial growth.

Towards Competitive Performance

The imperative of improved performance has serious implications for India if it is to survive, stay abreast and succeed. It calls for national efforts on systemic efficiency and productivity growth, the move from an investment-driven to an innovation-driven economy and sustained higher-order competitiveness; towards enhanced customer satisfaction at home and penetration of selected markets abroad. Concurrently, governments and business have to address such intractable problems as poverty, corruption and the degradation of the environment.

Creating New Technology-based Ventures

Starting a new business in India is a hazardous task. Problems are compounded when the venture is technology-based:

- Capital requirements are generally larger, while traditional banks are ill-equipped to process the perceived risk. Venture capital generally only becomes an option when the venture has documented the merits of its management, market and innovation.
- Knowledge-based ventures can benefit from linkages to sources of knowledge—e.g. the technical university or research lab. Such mentoring needs to be cultivated.
- Techno-entrepreneurs often have technical skills but usually lack the business management and marketing skills necessary for success. These need to be supplemented.
- In fields where technology is changing rapidly, it is often advantageous to make technology-acquisition arrangements. Sourcing such innovations, negotiating technology licensing agreements and protecting the intellectual property itself require special skills.
- Knowledge-based innovations are inherently more risky than others. The management of this unique risk requires assessment techniques and vision.

- Technology-based ventures often have social and environmental implications, which need to be managed carefully.
- Penetrating a competitive market requires good market intelligence, a good strategic plan and good luck.

Special Characteristics of "Techno-entrepreneurs"

The popular misconceptions are that techno-entrepreneurs are born, not made; that they take risks with other people's money and fail more often than they succeed. In fact, entrepreneur skills can be identified and developed. The entrepreneur is typically an innovator who formulates new solutions to existing problems, mobilizes resources and stimulates others to participate in his or her team. These aptitudes develop over time, often starting in childhood, as the person faces new challenges and learns from failure.

Entrepreneurial opportunities can be found in every industrializing country, community and family. Principal sources of entrepreneurs for knowledge-based ventures are often the university and government research laboratories, the large industrial and military establishments and professional service firms. Some motivations of the entrepreneur are the need to: be independent; create value; contribute to society; earn recognition; become rich or; quite often, simply not to be unemployed. Value-adding ventures with good growth potential can best be developed in an open market and in a culture which supports risk-taking.

The techno-entrepreneur anywhere has the challenge of moving a concept through the prototype and production phases towards creation of a product which meets market needs at a price consistent with the value created and with the ability of customers to pay.

Equally important, the market itself has to be developed and sustained. It is not enough to be first with a better mousetrap if one does not have the skills to educate and reach potential buyers and to set the market standard.

Hence one has to distinguish between innovators and inventors. The inventor is typically a creative person in a quest for knowledge or for producing new products, without determining in advance whether a real market exists for his or her inventions. On the other hand, the innovator draws on existing knowledge and the talents of others to develop or adapt a product or service at a volume and cost that can capture a significant portion of an identified market. The flexibility and creativity of a small entrepreneurial techno-venture may lead to more incremental and break-through innovations than can be generated by larger-sised firms in many sectors.

The pace and pattern of India's economic development now depend in large measure on its technical resource base. In this context, the key determinants are the skills to apply technology for enhanced competitiveness, as well as to create techbased ventures. Techno-entrepreneurs have to be supported by appropriate national structures and international linkages if they are to survive and flourish in an intensely competitive world.

15
Challenging Traditional Economic Growth

Today, saving the planet is about redefining our economic development models. Stirving towards the fulfilment of basic human rights is an integral part of environmental protection. Without a people-centred development strategy we will fail. Conflicting interests and lack of vision and courage are among the many reasons why it is so hard to meet needs in a world of plenty. We are faced with three major challenges in the 1990s.

- Top curb population growth and poverty.
- To search for sustainable production and consumption patterns.
- To promote equity.

Population growth is often associated with poverty. But who causes the major strain on the environment? The 1.2 billion poorest people consume small amounts of the world's resources and contribute little to harmful emissions. They do not cause a heavy burden. The day-to-day struggle for survival of the poorest does, however, undermine their resources, and this causes deaths as population grows beyond the carrying capacity of nature. Here two key elements are essential: to turn from non-renewable to renewable resources, and to minize use of resources through resource efficiency. We must single out the products and processes that must be phased out and those which may be allowed to expand. Right prices that include the ecological costs will be explored further, together with administrative measures. We are ready to examine the possibilities of using "geen tax" reforms to enhance employment and harness pollution and inefficient resources use. By shifting the burden of taxes from labour to environmentally harmful products and processes we might achieve a double benefit.

Transport, waste management, energy and land use are obvious areas that need to be affected by policy changes. Individuals must use their power as green-conscious citizens and shoppers—but, in the end, producers and service providers hold the main key to practical action.

The market must be harnessed to meet people's needs both for present and future generations—starting by making economic policies play by the rules of nature. The World Trade Organisation (WTO) negotiations have provided us with instruments to regulate world trade.

Getting the Prices Right

Car emissions may be cut drastically, but the rapid increase of new cars nullifies the benefits. Even the most ardent technological optimist must admit that we need new priorities or cuts in some products and services. For example, we must improve public transport and resource-efficient cars—and reduce traffic.

Traditional economic growth models fall short of solving the problem of unemployment. Indeed, 'robots' and wasteful resource use replace people. There are great job-creating possibilities in environment-friendly produces and processes. Striving towards equity within and between nations, and within and between generations, is the major challenge of our time.

The fact that 20 per cent of the world's population consumes 80 per cent of the world's resources has too long been seen as mainly an ethical challenge. Ethics are not easily translated into politics, especially when confronted with economic and market realities. As equity gradually becomes a security issue—as it will, if we do not bridge the gaps within and between nations—it will climb to the top of the political agenda.

Many of the main conflict areas of today are battlefields of resource management. These will expand greatly if we do not turn conference statements of good intention into action. The 30 year old commitment of the rich countries to meet the target of 0.7 per cent of GNP in official Development Assistance remains unmet.

Two hundred years of Western-led development optimism reached its peak in the late 1980s. When the Berlin wall fell, the economic growth models of the rich countries had become the universal recipe. But as more and more people aspire to join the ranks of the middle classes, the resulting environmental stress calls for a halt, or a radical change of course.

The call for new patterns of production and consumption challenges our traditional concepts of economic growth and the focus on materialism in our culture. Neither the industrialised nor the poorer countries are strangers to radical process of change, though the reasons for change are shifting. And we are truly facing challenging and conflict-providing changes.

No nation by itself can solve the problems we face. Pollution knows no frontiers, but comes to us with the winds and waves. We have become more and more interdependent. If we are to attain sustainable development, we must commit ourselves through international agreements, through an international rule of law, through the development of financial mechanisms and through institutional agreements. We must develop means and tools to enhance collective security and mutual interests.

16

Can Economic Growth Reduce Poverty?

New Findings on Inequality, Economic Growth and Poverty

Many people still think first of 'economic growth' in relation to poverty reduction. Indeed, their correlation is one of the mot-discussed issues of combating poverty. The relationship is of great importance because if there is a clear causal dependency, reducing poverty could fundamentally be limited to measures to promote growth. However, if there was low growth or stagnation if would not be possible to reduce poverty decisively. In the opposite case, that of the phenomena having no causal relation, promising measures to reduce poverty could be taken up even without economic growth.

Hardly anyone now explicitly expresses the view that economic development trickles down automatically to the poor. Practical experience has refuted this assumption dating from the early days of development policy in the 1960s. However, a number of studies show development of growth and a decline in poverty running parallel. On the other hand, there are also examples which show that despite high economic growth, poverty is not reduced markedly. The common answer to the question this raises is thus: Yes, growth can reduce poverty, but only if additional measures oriented on the poor are taken up. This is often termed pro-poor-growth. But what that means in detail, and whether economic growth as such plays a causal role at all, is not clarified. It is worth taking a look at the arguments on the basis of more recent empirical and theoretical knowledge.

No Direct Causality Between Growth and Poverty Reduction

Among the many indicators of poverty, the income of the

poor (income poverty) has the closest relationship to economic growth. An increase in gross domestic product and thus national income could, if other factors come into play be linked with an increase in the per capita income of the poor.

Such a relationship between economic growth and the income of the poor, however, cannot be described as causal, as is asserted implicitly time and again by the statement that growth is a necessary but not sufficient precondition for poverty reduction. In so far as growth and poverty reduction arise at the same time at the end of a process, they exist alongside each other. It would be almost a tautology to say that the former is the cause or part-cause of the latter. Both express the same thing, namely a change in per capita income as well, and both have similar causes. What matters is recognising what these causes are and what specific factors must come into play so that the income of the poor grows too. Growth as a "prerequisite" or "condition" is then no longer the focus; the priority is asking for specific policies that result in higher incomes for the poor. The detour in thinking about growth is not necessary. Since, however, it is based on similar factors, such as fiscal policy/ budget structure, employment policy, combating inflation, and institutional development, economic growth can also emerge if poverty is reduced. The difference of views lies in the fact that under the heading 'poverty reduction' the aim is no longer growth, but a purposeful reduction of poverty.

Therefore, in reverse, successful combating of poverty can be seen as being the cause of growth insofar as activating the capabilities of the poor and using their productive capacity of the poor and using their productive capacity triggers economic drive.

Indirect Causality Between Growth and Poverty Reduction?

So even if economic growth fundamentally has no direct causal impact on poverty, growth still can reduce it indirectly. This is the case when due to positive economic development a government has greater revenue and uses the surplus for combating poverty, for example by providing such public goods as education and health services. Also in these cases, however, growth is not a compelling precondition. Even without growth greater government revenue can be achieved for example by more efficient tax collection. And leeway for social welfare spending can be gained by redistributing the budget, such as by cutting military appropriations. Furthermore, an automatic process is not given because the government can also use surplus funds for non-social purposes.

Creation of jobs due to increased economic activity can be another indirect link between economic growth and income poverty, if such a development generates income and reduces poverty. But also in this case I see no compelling causality because, for instance, industrial jobs are not necessarily open to the really poor. In addition, these positive impacts occur to a considerable extent only in the event of labour-intensive development. In many countries, however, economic growth is achieved by capital-intensive production.

Inequality, Growth and Income Poverty

If national incomes, grow, a naïve observer might assume that the income of the poor must also grow along with it. But that would be a statistical fallacy. Even if only the income of the rich grows, this results in macroeconomics statistics showing a higher per capita income. What the true conditions are is shown as soon as one divides the population statistically into income groups, such as in fifths, as is usual. It then turns out that the bald figures on average per capita growth can certainly cloak a situation where the income of the richest fifth of the population is growing fast while that of the poorest fifth is stagnating. Despite growth, the gap between the two becomes even wider.

The unequal distribution of income (and of other assets such as property and access to social services), and its connection to poverty reduction and growth has recently returned to the forefront of the debate.

It is obvious that inequality and its changes have direct effects on the poverty situation. Does inequality also have an impact on poverty via its relation to growth, because growth promotes or reduces inequality? Earlier, the predominant view was that rapid growth was linked with at least a temporary increase in inequality, so that a distinct policy of growth initially disadvantaged the poor.

The current dominant view is that growth has no foreseeable effects on inequality and that inequality changes only very slowly, in reverse, however, it is assumed that greater equality is a determinant of growth. According to that view, an indirect relationship between poverty on one side and inequality as a factor dependent upon growth on the other is not given.

That leads to the conclusion that fair distribution has more weight than growth. Fair distribution, however, does not depend upon growth. An appropriate policy is possible at any time, not only after an economic situation has improved. The notion that still shimmers through the debate that "something must be earned first before it can be distributed", is wrong. It is a matter of designing policy and the entire economic process right from the start in such a way that the surplus benefits all including the poor. Important elements of such a policy are, for example, land reform and development of finance systems.

Relationship of Growth to Poverty

According to today's conventional wisdom, income poverty expresses only a part of what poverty means. Not least through the voices of the poor themselves, it has become clear that violation of human dignity and rights, a lack of participation in decisions and exclusion from society, unequal treatment of men and women, and vulnerability are also regarded as poverty. For poverty is caused to a great degree by conflicts of power and interests. Income poverty often is not even seen as the greatest problem.

What relationship do these more far reaching characteristics of poverty have to economic growth? A direct relationship of growth to socially-related aspects such as women's inheritance rights, land rights and exclusion from decisions cannot be seen. Considerable improvements in favour of the poor can be achieved here even without economic growth.

Those who see a strong and causal connection between economic growth and poverty reduction must ask themselves what the prospects are for high growth rates and thus for decline in poverty. Coupling poverty reduction to economic growth is problematic. If only low growth rates are to be expected.

Another question is whether continuous increases in growth are at all desirable and possible in the medium to long term. In this connection, a difference should perhaps be made between developing countries and industrialised nations. But environmental compatibility and availability of resources set limits to growth for both. Some academics assume that industrialised nations have already reached an inherent limit (stagnation theory) and that the high growth rates of earlier years will not return. Moreover, they add, full employment is no longer achievable due to, among other things, an ongoing increase in productivity, and current unemployment cannot be reduced by customary means. In any case, if growth were to be taken as the major benchmark, the prospects for a radical reduction of income poverty around the world would be modest.

Summing Up

Poverty is a complex problem and reducing it depends upon many interconnected factors that is why poverty cannot be attributed to one main cause nor its reduction based on one main strategy. Economic growth is just one strategic element among many others related to poverty reduction. An indirect causal connection between growth and poverty reduction can only be seen because governments will have a grater scope for action due to economic growth, and if they promote labour-intensive development.

Therefore growth's role in poverty reduction must be put into perspective Growth cannot be the first thing that comes to mind, nor is it the golden path to reducing poverty. The simplistic theory of economic growth as the main condition obstructs the bigger picture; it clings to the underlying and ongoing belief in the trickle-down effect. Even if there is no growth or for inherent reasons there can be none, there are promising ways to take on the challenge of mass poverty in the developing countries. Up front, governments and bilateral and multilateral donors must have the political will to design economic, financial and social policies so that they are oriented on poverty in a coherent way—the result can also be economic growth.

17

High World Trade Growth Vs. Output: *WTO Sees Link to Globalisation*

World trade in merchandise goods is expected to increase in volume by 8 per cent in 1995 down marginally on the very high 9½ per cent for 1994. Although the current outlook is for a further modest slowing next year, trade growth will remain above the average of the past decade.

Recent trade growth figures continue to exceed world production growth by a large margin in 1995 probably by a factor of almost three and next year close to double. This persistent pattern relates closely to the "globalization" of the world economy; a processes which, brings far-reaching benefits and which can be promoted through the further development of the multilateral trading system.

The recent growth is as follows:

- a 13 per cent rise pushed the value of world merchandise trade past the $4,000 billion mark for the first time, to $4,090 billion.
- an 8 per cent increase in the value of trade in commercial services, to $1,100 billion, after near stagnation in 1993;
- a 23 per cent increase in the dollar value of merchandise trade in the first six months of 1995 which, allowing for the depreciation of the US dollar, is consistent with a full-year growth in trade volume of 8 per cent.

Globalisation

Over the period from 1950 when the process of trade liberalisation through the early GATT Round got under-way to 1994, the volume of world merchandise trade increased at an annual rate of slightly more than 6 per cent and world output by close to 4 per cent. Thus, during those 45 years world merchandise trade multiplied 14 times and output 5½ times. However, the excess of trade growth over output growth varied; from an average of a mere half percentage point in the period 1974-84 to nearly 3½ percentage points in the most recent 10 years. In fact, the excess during the years since 1990 has been much higher still but it is not yet clear whether or not this represents a permanent shift to a faster rate of increase in the world's trade-to-output ratio.

To the question "will globalisation continue?" In this regard one has to observe two factors—technological change and the evolving strategies of firms and individual investors—impart a natural momentum to global integration. It is government policies which can speed-up, slow down or even reverse progress on global integration. In this context, the role of non-discrimination—in particular, through the "most-favoured-nation" (MFN) clause—is examined.

The MFN Clause

MFN was the centrepiece of a multiplicity of bilateral trade agreements reached in Europe in the second half of the 19th century, a period marked by very low tariffs and rapidly increasing trade. In contrast, the 1920s and the 1930s saw effects to restore liberal trade through international trade conferences rather than legally-binding commercial treaties based on MFN. The failure of these efforts contributed to the Great Depression and provided some of the roots of military confrontation in 1939. It was only after the War that negotiations established what became the GATT, a multilateral contract consisting of rules and disciplines and based firmly (Article) on MFN treatment.

The GATT system has been a post-war bulwark against a return to the trade chaos of the 1930's. In the 1990's, a disintegration of the globalised international economy on the scale of 1930's is almost unthinkable. In contrast, today "the threat that would be posed by a loss of credibility of the multilateral rules" (now represented by the WTO) would be "a fracturing of the global economy into inward-looking and potentially antagonistic trading blocks".

One can suggest two safeguards against such an eventually:

- the examination of new ways to ensure that free-trade areas and customs unions remain outward-looking and complement rather than compete with the multilateral trading system; and
- progress in dealing, at the multilateral level, with new issues tied directly to the further evolution of the global economy. These include telecommunications, financial services, environment, competition and investment policies among others.

Progress in dealing with these and other issues at the multilateral level will have a significant impact on the future pace of global integration, both directly and through its impact on the credibility of the multilateral system in influencing the broad spectrum of national trade policies.

18

What's Driving Migration

The scale and diversity of today's migrations are beyond any previous experience. Rapid urban growth and environmental degradation in rural areas have led to internal migration affecting hundreds of million of people. Migration is now seen as a priority issue equal in political weight to other major global challenges such as the environment, population growth and economic imbalances between regions.

Families and households form the basis for economic growth, social development and personal fulfilment. Decisions, by individual women and men on marriage, family, a place to live, shape the destinies of communities and nations. National policies and international conditions provide the context for individual decision-making. Effective development policies, including population, reproductive health and family planning policies, address this reality.

Data on national and global population trends set the agenda for national policy. An important element of population programmes is gathering data that will allow policy-making responsive to the realities of daily life, and to the needs and aspirations of individuals.

The dominant feature of global demographics is still growth. Age distribution is a growing concern, as the numbers of young and elderly people, grow, relative to the working-age population. The world is growing steadily more urban. From being a sign of strength and dynamism in the national economy, the rate and scale of urban growth has become increasingly a cause for concern. The influx of migrants to the biggest cities may be weakening both urban and rural sectors.

International migration is small in extent compared with internal movements, but has a disproportionate impact. Both internal and international migration are driven by population growth, and by inequities between countries. Migration is one of the choices which shape people's lives and the destiny of nations. But it can also be a symptom of inequity and underdevelopment. Migrants are by definition the most vulnerable members of the host community. Their living and working conditions should be protected.

Open and frank exchange of information and views between host and sending countries is needed more than ever. The aim of the international community should be to protect the right to move, but to ensure that movement is voluntary and that it stimulates rather than holds back personal and national development. "The point of departure should be the human right to live and work where one pleases, so long as it does not infringe on other people's rights to do the same."

The Urban Transformation

The rural sector is declining in importance and its contribution to national economies. It is increasingly part of a unified economy based on the city. Contact with the urban areas is easier than ever and is encouraged by rural development.

Temporary and circular migration is giving way to more permanent settlement. The largest cities are under increasing strain, and residents are encountering increasing difficulties in improving or even maintaining living conditions. Nevertheless, migration continues, driven by a variety of forces both positive and negative. The choice to move can be part of a strategy for survival or personal development; but it is often enforced by external conditions.

The urban transformation is irreversible, but the rural sectors must also be strengthened to balance the developing economy. Attention to gender issues will be crucial in ensuring a successful transition. The forces driving internal and international migration have much in common. Demographic pressures are contributing to both. As the pressures encouraging migration increase, the options for migrants become more limited. This collision is contributing to the atmosphere of crisis surrounding both urban and international migration.

Costs and Benefits

Migration is the result of individual or family decisions. But it is also part of social process. In economic terms, migration is as much a global phenomenon as trade in commodities or manufactured goods. It is part of a broader pattern, and evidence of changing economic, social and cultural relationships.

But migration may be evidence of a different kind of relationship; the combination of poverty, rapid population growth and environmental damage is a powerful destabilizing factor driving urban growth and eventually international migration. On the recipient side, migration has usually been seen as evidence of a thriving economy: today's industrial states were built in part by migrant labour, skills and investment. In today's increasingly uncertain conditions, migration may be seen as a threat to the security and well-being of the local workforce and society at large.

The only effective means to reduce migration pressures over the long term are to slow population growth; to stimulate economic growth and job creation at home, and promote the development of the individual and the family as the basic economic and social unit.

A Question of Gender

It is often assumed that most migrants are men, in reality, women make up nearly half of the international migrant population. Gender differences in social and economic roles affect migration decision making, household strategy, and the sex composition of labour migration. Attention to the gender dimension of migratory movements ought to be an important component in population and development planning.

Women frequently take the initiative in migration decisions, which may reflect limited opportunities in rural areas. Low status limits women's choices at home and may increase pressure to migrate, but it may also affect life in the host community. Opportunities may be limited by lack of education or skills, or by customer limitation on women's freedom of action outside the family or ethnic group. Paid employment for migrant women is usually in the lowest wage, least secure, and lowest status jobs, mostly in housework, child care and trade.

Most educated women end up in the same low-status, low-wage production and servicejobs as unskilled female migrants. Men too, experience downward mobility, but the contrast in the decline in women's employment status is far greater. Despite these disadvantages women migrants have become significant economic actors. Their status may be improved by migration, but the advantages are not clear-cut. Women's status as migrants is affected by their vulnerability, and by their lack of reproductive freedom. To ensure improved status they will need both legal protection and essential services, including reproductive health services.

Refugees

Refugees in the 1990s are overwhelmingly in Asia, Africa and Latin America. Their numbers are large, about 17 million, and growing rapidly. A further 3.5 to 4 million were thought to be in "refugee-like situation", though estimates are probably extremely conservative, and an estimated 23 million people internally displaced.

It is important to recognize the common roots of refugees and other forms of mass movement of populations. At the same time, despite the difficulty of distinguishing between political and socio-economic causes of migration, there is a clear need to distinguish between refugees and other groups of migrants. Participation in international efforts of burden-sharing would ensure that most refugee problems would be dealt with in their regions of origin.

Conclusions and Policies

Migration highlights linkages and interdependencies within countries, with many implications for development agendas, including population programmes and development assistance.

Policies to regulate or moderate international migration have concentrated largely on urban growth. They have been only intermittently effective. The most successful have concentrated on stimulating rural development and the growth of alternative urban centres

Migration is also a personal or family decision, which is affected by external conditions such as poverty or environmental degradation, improving conditions of personal and family life can make a crucial difference in the decision to migrate, reducing dependence on migration as a strategy. Because migration is the result of personal and family decisions, it can be influenced by policies that improve the quality of life.

This offers the opportunity for policies emphasizing individual development, among them education, health (including reproductive health) and family planning. Such policies are particularly relevant to the Strategies must take into account gender differences in social and economic life and the differential effects of policies.

Migration decisions are about family security and long-term-life-chances, rather than simply the maximisation of income. They are ultimately strategies designed to look after the individual's and the house-hold's needs, safeguard their security, and respond to their aspirations. If the goal is to reduce migration pressures through development it will be essential to increase the capacity but reduce the need to migrate. Long-term external support will be required to make such policies a reality, particularly in areas of rapid population growth and potential mass outward flows. Highly co-ordinated allocation of development assistance can help establish priorities and focus attention on basic needs. The challenge to both international donors and co-operating governments is to direct programme spending to the areas where it can be most effective.

19

Income Gap Widens

The gap in income among the people of the world has been widening. In 1960, according to United Nations statisticians, the richest 20 per cent of the world's people received 30 times more income than the poorest 20 per cent. By 1991, they were getting 61 times more. While the poorest one-fifth in 1960 received a meagre 2.3 per cent of world income, by 1991 that revenue share had fallen to 1.4 per cent. The income share of the richest fifth, meanwhile, rose from 70 per cent to 85 per cent.

These disparities prevail both among countries and within them, and the large gap between individuals world wide reflects the combination of both of those splits. Almost four fifths of all people live in the developing world, where incomes are only fraction of those in industrial countries. In turn, within countries in both categories, gaps in income between citizens can be even wider.

The widest income gap reported within a country is in Botswana, where during the 1980s the richest 20 per cent of society received over 47 times more income than the poorest 20 per cent. Brazil was second, with a ratio of 32 to 1. In Guatemala and Panama, the ratio stood at 30 to 1.

The rapidly growing economies of East Asia have had income patterns similar to those of Western Europe and North America, with the richest one-fifth often earning 5 to 10 times more than the poorest fifth. In South Asia, India, Bangladesh, and Pakistan have had relatively even distributions of income, with the richest 20 per cent getting only four to five times more than the poorest quintile. Some countries that have had military conflicts apparently based in part on inequities among citizens, never the less have relatively even income distributions.

The split between countries and people can be seen in the marketplace. The value of luxury goods sales world-wide—high-fashion clothing and top-of-the-line autos, for example-exceeds the gross national products of two-thirds of the world's countries. The world's average income, roughly $4,000 a year, is well below the US poverty line.

The poorest fifth of the world accounted for 0.9 per cent of world trade, 1.1 per cent of global domestic investment, 0.9 per cent of global domestic savings, and just 0.2 per cent of global commercial credit at the beginning of the 1990s. Each of those shares declined between 1960 and 1990.

These disparities are reflected in the consumption of many resources. At the start of this decade, industrial countries home to roughly a fifth of the world's population, accounted for about 86 per cent of the consumption of aluminium, and chemicals, 81 per cent of the paper, 80 per cent of the iron and steel, and three-quarters of the timber and energy. Since then, economic growth in developing countries has probably reduced these percentages. China's economy, for example, is more than 50 per cent larger now than it was in 1990, and developing countries have passed industrial ones in fertilizer consumption.

Uneven income distribution is shaping some of the most important trends in the world today. It raises crime rates, for example. And it drives migration. People have long responded to economic disparities by following a patch from poor regions to richer ones, as tens of millions of workers chase higher wages and better opportunities. Some 1.6 million Asians and Middle Easterners were working in Kuwait and Saudi Arabia before they fled war in 1991, and at least 2.5 million Mexicans live in the United States.

The same is true within countries: rising disparities of income are adding to the growth of cities thorough rural to urban migration. Latin America, with some of the highest disparities of income among its citizens, is also the most urbanised region of the developing world-not entirely by coincidence. Since 1950, city dwellers there have risen from 42 per cent of the population to 73 per cent.

For many years, china had one of the most equal distributions of income in the world. But now that is changing, as income in its southern provinces and special economic zones soar while those in rural areas rise much more slowly. Also not coincidentally, the Chinese National Academy of Social Sciences forecasts that by 2010, half the population will live in cities, compared with 28 per cent today and only 10 per cent in the early 1980s.

In the early 1990s, developing world economies, especially, in East Asia, have grown faster than the economies of the industrial countries. This has the potential to shrink disparities of income, if poorer countries continue to catch up. Yet even if the gaps among countries narrow, the gaps between people may not, because economic growth is distributed so unevenly within nations. Despite the recent restoration of economic growth in Latin America, no progress is expected in reducing poverty, which is even likely to increase slightly.

Meanwhile, in some regions almost no one has been getting richer. The per capita income of most sub Saharan African nations actually fell during the 1980's. In sub-Sahaan Africa, the poorest geographic region, an estimated one-third of all a college graduates have left the continent. That loss of talented people, due in large part to poverty and a lack of opportunities in Africa, will make it even more difficult for the continent to advance.

The economic growth that has the potential to close income gaps among people in the developing world is instead become a splitting off, with some parts of societies joining the industrial world while others remain behind. Singapore, Hongkong, and Taiwan have begun to look like wealthy industrial countries, for example. Now parts of China are following, as are the wealthier segments of Latin American society and of Southeast Asian countries. This is good news for members of the middle-income countries and for the world. But it may do little to help the poorest fifth of humanity.

20

Policy Researchers and Policy Makers: *Never the Twain Shall Meet?*

In every corner of the planet, researchers are gathering and analyzing information on vital issues of sustainable development. But how do they know that their findings will actually be used in policy decisions that create positive change? Researchers and decision makers see the world, and their roles in it, in very different ways. What creates this divide between the two communities and what can be done to bridge the gap?

Demand-Side' Challenges: Policy in the Making

By its nature, the policy making process constrains decision makers from effectively expressing demands for research. Rigorous research requires a clear definition of a problem and the variables to be measured. But the objectives of government policies and programmes tend to be loosely defined and even contradictory. Many decisions are reached through a multilateral bargaining process in which it is difficult to obtain consensus on anything more than broad statements of principle. These bargains might break down if the costs and tradeoffs involved were exposed by a research project.

Inertia and more urgent priorities mean that government tend to think about changing policies only when time and funding have run out. At that point, it is too late for research. furthermore, it is only after a programme has been established and a clientele created that an effective demand exists for research. For these reasons, policy implementation tends to precede rather than follow research.

Even if there is a need for research, there may not be a single agency responsible for the policy decision bargaining. When a client agency does request advice, there is no guarantee that it will turn out to be the appropriate audience for the results (e.g. a study done for the ministry of education might find that student performance would be improved by better nutrition).

Finally, governments are often afflicted with too much information, which senior policy makers have little time to absorb.

'Supply Side' Challenges of Academic Research

Problems also exist in the research community that supplies information and analysis. University research usually takes a long time to yield results. It is often highly critical, without suggestions for action, but fitting the self-image of many academics a gadflies. In academia, a state of conflicting views and information is normal. But potential clients find their confidence undermined when two studies reach opposite conclusions.

Academics often search for general laws and patterns that reveal phenomena of greater theoretical and long run importance than highly specific observations. Policy makers, however, want answers to the specific problems they face, even if such 'small' problems do not interest researchers.

While policy makers tend to emphasize distributional concerns (i.e. winners and losers) and the number of people affected, economists—frequent advisors to government—emphasize efficiency and financial costs and benefits. Owing party to the vagueness of many programme goal, policy makers tend to assess performance in terms of inputs rather than improvements in health. They also weigh losses more heavily than gains, since "a policy that hurts five people and helps five, produces five enemies and five ingrates".

Finally, the issue of compensation is critical to policy makers; for economists it is usually an afterthought. Economists tend to find a solution satisfactory if, in theory, the losers could be compensated. To push a policy change through, policy makers must usually ensure that they will be compensated, and have mechanisms to do so.

Impact Down the Road

The gap between demand and supply for research appears rather large. But this view may be too pessimistic, mainly because it uses narrow definitions of research and policy impact. Research is more than a set of data and policy impact may accumulate imperceptibly but with real effect over many years. The contribution of social science research is perhaps less in proposing specific solutions to well-defined problems, than in defining the problems and providing an array of concepts and methods for analysis.

Problem definition can take many forms. It can mean detecting problems for patterns in data, such as a trend toward worsening income distribution. It can also change the way society thinks about issues. Largely because of research, the informal sector now tends to be seen as a potential force for development, rather than a symptom of backwardness.

The most significant contribution of social science research may be in generating ideas and ideologies, which history shows can be very powerful.

What to do?

How, then, can researchers and the agencies that sponsor them increase the social relevance and impact of research? Since both the problem-solving and the conceptual impacts are important, research programmes should be designed to provide both by developing an understanding of basic behavioural relationship and a thorough knowledge of the data. This can then be tapped to provide short-term policy advice.

Donors have an important role to play in supporting theoretical research, although they are sometimes reluctant to do so. The distinction between "theoretical" and "empirical" is in no sense equivalent to "useless" and "useful". A plausible, verifiable theory about how farmers respond to increase in crop prices, or savings to changes in interest rates, is of obvious relevance to poverty and can be very useful.

Greater attention should go to publicizing findings and donors should be prepared to finance conferences, books, working papers, abstracts and the like. Researchers should convey their findings in language intelligible to practitioners, putting themselves into policy makers' shoes when doing so. Among the recommendations made by successful policy advisors are the following

- learn about the history of the issue by researching previous arguments, interest groups, areas of disagreement and data gaps;
- get into the debate early before positions harden;
- explain which groups will be affected by the proposed measures and suggest ways to compensate those negatively affected;
- do not propose measures that are technically optimal but too complex or costly for an agency to administer; and
- keep it simple. Emphasize the decision at hand, the underlying problem, and options to solve it. Minimize methodology, jargon and equations.

In the research domain, there is no single recipe for policy impact. Luck and persistence, along with good science, are vital ingredients.

21

Crisis Prevention: *Can Better Development Planning Lessen the Toll of Civil Emergencies and Natural Disasters?*

Even a cursory scan of the world's headlines is depressing: armed conflicts are grinding on in Somalia, Afghanistan and in a growing number of other countries. And the effects of natural disasters are becoming more catastrophic each year. International relief aid, in response to such emergencies, has increased substantially. But how large can these sums of money realistically be expected to grow? With no end in sight to the need for relief, the good will of international donors is quickly giving way to disillusionment.

This leads us to a second question, which is, where does development fit in this grim scenario? For the development community to remain aloof from the issue of disasters and emergencies is not only politically short-sighted, it also ignores totally the causes and the effects of such phenomena.

Natural hazards such as hurricanes and earthquakes may be impossible to prevent. But they only become natural disasters if people are vulnerable. Why is it, for example, that an earthquake in Khilari, Maharashtra that registered 6.9 on the Richter scale killed up to 35,000 people, when an earthquake of almost the exact same magnitude in Los Angeles in 1994 claimed only 57 lives? By reducing poverty we can help increase, the coping capacity of vulnerable populations. Therefore helping people lower such vulnerability is as much a development issue as the environment, or women's participation in development.

Moreover, the repercussions of natural disasters go far beyond the immediate casualty list that so transfixes the media. Secondary and longer-term effects can be equally if not more devastating. And they must be taken into account by developing practitioners.

It has been estimated, for example, that the damage to Mexico City's infrastructure form a massive 1985 earthquake amounted to US$ 3.6 billion. Yet over the subsequent five years, the negative ripple effect on that country's balance of payments resulted in a loss of $8.6 billion. Furthermore, reconstruction requirements forced Mexican authorities to revise their economic policies to meet an increased demand for public funding, credits and imports. The priorities for public expenditure were redirected to reconstruction projects, leaving many of the pre-disaster problems of the city and its people unattended.

In Bangladesh, floods in the recent past 2,000 people. But on closer examination we find that the toll was much more expensive than that: in each of these years the country's economic growth rate was halved by the delayed planting of rice and the destruction of seedbeds in the floods, further undermining the country's food security. All of these are consideration that go beyond relief, but they must be taken into account by development professionals.

Other emergencies may be more complex, but must be subjected to the same analysis. As the situations in Angola, Burundi, Somalia and the former Yugoslavia demonstrate, we know little about the dynamics of emergencies that arise from civil conflict. We do know, however that their cause usually lies in a lethal mix of poverty, poor governance and ethnic or religious rivalries exacerbated by profound social inequities. We are also learning that their resolution frequently requires the application of peacekeeping and political measures, combined with relief and development. Among the most virulent effects of such complex emergencies is the massive displacement of people; women and children are the principal victims, constituting 70 per cent of the world's refugees.

These complex emergencies around the world could easily get worse before they get better. This being said, carefully designed development efforts-carried out as building blocks to national reconciliation in the fragile post-conflict stagewill need to increase commensurately. The appropriateness and the sustainability of these development efforts will be one of the most important factors in determining whether peace itself becomes sustainable. For example, the absence of carefully tailored reintegration strategies for demobilised soldiers and their host communities would be an almost open invitation to resumed violence.

Yet we must also be conscious of the impact of aid and try harder to prevent the need for relief in the first place. An increasing body of evidence suggests for example that emergency aid can sometimes be counter-productive in the longer term, increasing the vulnerability of populations and impeding recovery. Ironically, we find ourselves in situation today where it is far easier to obtain funds for maintaining refugees in their places of asylum than for helping them reintegrate into their own societies. In such cases, we may very well be helping to perpetuate the problem that we sought to relieve, as the presence of large numbers of refugees is sometimes itself a cause of conflict.

So how are we to proceed? And what exactly is the nature of the relief to development continuum that remains logical in the abstract but elusive in reality? The concept of a continuum does not imply a linear and absolutely progressive set of responses. On the contrary, it means that we are dealing with a set of processes rather than rigidly defined steps. It also means that development must be very much part of the disaster management process, and that the aim of the continuum must be to move from relief to rehabilitation and resumed development at the earliest opportunity. However, this resumed development must include conscious measures to reduce the vulnerability that caused the disaster or the emergency in the first place.

In other words, we must give greater thought to prevention before we reach for the "cure"—for humanitarian, political and financial reasons. (The Japanese insurance industry spends $200 million a year on disaster education alone). And as development practitioners, we must reconcile ourselves to the vastly more complicated environment in which we have to operate.

This means, for example that we will have to begin examining whether the economic policy "medicine" often prescribed will reduce conflict or enhance it. We will have to ask ourselves if the reconstruction period following a civil conflict or natural disaster is the right time to advocate cuts in social spending, as has happened in certain countries in Africa and Latin America. Similarly, is it really in children's best interests to build a school in a seismic zone without first ensuring its structural stability? And does it really make sense to urge drought-prone countries to increase their reliance on cash crops, as has been done in some instances.

A story that never made headlines anywhere involves hundreds of the poorest people in Bangladesh, whose homes remained intact during the floods of 1988, when many others were simply washed away. These people were fortunate enough to have obtained credit through the Grameen Bank for construction materials as well as instruction in the building of flood-resistant homes. The Grameen revolving fund had received start-up capital from International Financial Agencies. Since that time the effort has been expanded, and more than 10,500 flood-resistant homes have been built in the last two years.

This is just one example of the kind of action we need more of—in fairly predictable and recurring circumstances such as the floods in Bangladesh, as well as in the more complex, man-made emergencies to which we must respond.

22

Money Alone is Not Enough: *Technology Transfer and Environmental Protection*

In the seventies it was a hotly debated topic, in the eighties it became a moot issue: The demand of the developing countries for low-cost or even free technology transfers from the industrial nations. The environment, or more accurately, the endangered environment, is responsible for reviving this subject once believed to be dead. Politicians in the South were quick to see the opportunity which presented itself: No environmental protection without technology, no technology without technology transfer, not technology transfer without money.

The Montreal treaty (on the reduction of chlorofluorocarbon production) was an important first step. It established a fund which supports the environmental efforts of the developing countries. But this was only the beginning. Technology was one of the main concerns of the United Nations Conference on Environment and Development (UNCED).

It is undisputed that private enterprises control the expertise necessary for environmentally sound technologies. The discussions in the developing countries revolve around this basic issue: What guarantees are there that these firms will transfer any technologies at all and at an acceptable price to boot? Both premises present a problem: in all likelihood, technology monopolists have invested substantial amounts in the development of the respective technology and will therefore try to sell their licenses at the highest possible price (price problem). Having had so many failures with specific projects in the past, many firms are not quite reluctant to transfer technology to the developing countries. It was no coincidence that north-South technology transfers practically came to a standstill in the eighties.

Technology cannot be purchased as a package. This is a frequently forgotten truism. By general definition, technology consists of four components:

- Hardware, for instance a specific configuration of machines and equipment to manufacture a product or provide a service;
- Know-how, i.e. scientific and technical knowledge, qualifications, and empirical knowledge;
- Organization, i.e. the arrangement which combines hardware, know-how, and operational management methods;
- The end product, i.e. the item or service.

The technical components (machines, blueprints) and products (licenses) can be purchased subject to the cited restrictions, but not organisation and qualifications. This is the real bottleneck for technological development in most developing countries. There is not inductive to the process which is most important for the utilisation of technology technological learning.

The core of technological knowledge is the mastery and subsequent continuous improvement of production processes. In part this happens automatically (learning by doing), but beyond that it must be actively stimulated. Many examples in both industrial and developing countries show that firms frequently stagnate at a certain technological level, thus missing a chance to improve efficiency. The main reason is inadequate technological knowledge. The secret of optimizing the conversion process lies in a strategy of small steps, the steady improvement of individual segments.

The economically most dynamic developing countries are successful because of high productivity increases made possible by technological competence, i.e. the ability to assess and evaluate the technology offer, to select, utilize, and improve technologies, and ultimately develop new ones. This latest state-of-the art processes can be used for industrial expansion projects. As far as these countries are concerned, the introduction of financing mechanisms for the transfer of environmentally sound technologies represents a very promising approach.

Technological Competence the Crucial Factor

In other countries industrialisation efforts have caused serious environmental degradation but little economic development. The reason is last but not least inadequate, only slowly growing technological competence. Those countries have hardly any money to invest in environmentally sound technologies. But even if the international community establishes financing mechanism, the problem of inadequate technological competence remains unsolved. It is unreasonable to assume that in a country, where conventional production technologies are used ineffectively and inefficiently, environmentally sound technologies can suddenly be applied in a meaningful and efficient manner. For these countries the transfer of environmentally sound technologies is a "quick fix" which in all likelihood will not work. Without an established level of national technological competence, it will not do much good to shower a country with technology from outside (more precisely, with technical hardware and production know-how).

This brings us to an original development policy problem. Technology and technology transfer have always played a big role in development policy, although quite often the perspective was shortterm: Instead of technology, only hardware was transferred; frequently, technological competence was not developed in the recipient countries, but rather substituted with external experts. In the future, much more emphasis will have to be placed on stimulating the technological learning process and promoting national technological competence. Many developing countries have already moved in this direction, such as instituting macro-political reforms, which pressure private industry to increase performance, thus forcing technological learning. But development policy can make a contribution as well. Above all, it will have to adopt a more systemic approach and promote structural improvements at several levels:

- As a systemic link between project and project environment. Technology institutions have always been the darling of environmental policy, but frequently they had too little contact with potential users and therefore remained ineffective.

- As linkage with indigenous efforts in the recipient countries and with the activities of other donors. Isolated projects and competition among donors are a guarantee for failure. On the other hand, the fascination in many recipient countries with individual technologies is slowly being replaced by a growing understanding of the technological correlations, concerted technological political actions, which have already been initiated in some developing countries (for instance Thailand, Jordan and Tanzania) and which brought together representatives of government, private industry, educational and research institutions at "round table" discussions, provide an opportunity for the systemic incorporation of technologically oriented development policy measures:

A Dual Challenge for the Industrial Nations

The industrial nations are thus faced with a dual challenge. First, they must support those developing countries financially whose technological competence is adequate for the effective utilisation of environmentally sound technologies. On a global scale, this is an ecologically rewarding undertaking. Since environmental standards have been low in these countries, investments can achieve substantially higher reductions of pollutants than in the industrialised North. There is another aspect: The industrial nations can put pressure on the developing countries to use environmentally sound processes only if they simultaneously offer financial compensation. Secondly, the industrial nations must increase their efforts to raise the level of technological competence in developing countries. This is an essential pre-condition for the developing countries to be able to participate in the medium term in an environmentally benign growth model.

23

Population Growth and Income

Global economic output, the total of all goods, and services produced, grew from $5 trillion in 1950 to $29 trillion in 1998, expanding more than twice as fast as population. This increase of nearly sixfold boosted incomes rather substantially for most of humanity. Growth of the world economy from 1990 to 1997 exceeded the growth during the 10,000 years from the beginning of agriculture until 1950.

Economic output per person climbed from just over @ 1,900 in 1950 to nearly @ 5,000 in 1997, a gain of 163 per cent. Although there is an enormous income gap between industrial and developing countries, the latter's economies are growing far more rapidly. Growth in industrial countries has slowed to scarcely 2 per cent a year during the 1990s, compared with nearly 6 per cent a year in developing nations.

The fastest-growing region in the world from 1990, to 1997 was Asia, which averaged nearly 8 per cent annually. This growth was led by China, whose economy has been increasing at nearly 10 per cent a year throughout much of this decade, making it the world's fastest-growing economy. Since 1980, China's economic output has doubled every eight years.

Incomes have risen most rapidly in developing countries where population growth has slowed the most, including, importantly, the countries of East Asia-South Korea, Taiwan, China, Thailand, Indonesia, and Malaysia, concentrating early on reducing birth rates helped to boost savings to invest in education, health care, and the infrastructure needed by a modern industrial society.

At the other end of the spectrum, African countries—largely ignoring family planning—have been overwhelmed by the sheer numbers of young people who need to be educated and employed. With population growth rates remaining at close to 3 per cent or more a year, most of any economic growth that occurred has been absorbed by the increasing population, leaving little to raise incomes.

The enormous growth during the 1990s, particularly in East Asia, is due to the huge increase in private capital flows into developing countries. Between 1990 and 1997, annual private capital flows increased from $42 billion to $256 billion, a gain of more than sixfold. This substantial amount of money dwarfs traditional flows in public funds under international aid programmes.

Although incomes in much of the developing world are rising rapidly, they are not rising for everyone. The World Bank estimates that 1.3 billion of the world's people subsist on $1 a day or less. For this one fifth of humanity, trapped at a subhuman level of existence, there has not been any meaningful progress.

The sources of growth are changing. In earlier times, most of the growth was in agriculture. Since the advent of the Industrial Revolution, however, more and more of the growth has been concentrated in industry. Then beginning around mid-century, the services sector-insurance, banking, education-began to expand rapidly, accounting for most of the change in the industrial world. More recently, growth has been concentrated in the information sector as computerisation of the economy and telecommunciations have grown at extraordianry rates.

The good news is that the global economy has been expanding at a near record pace during the 1990, the bad news is that the economy, as now structured, is outgrowing the Earth's ecosystem. The result is excessive pressures on the natural systems and resources. As noted in the first section of this paper, from 1950 to 1997 the use of lumber more than doubled. That of paper increased sixfold, the fish catch increased nearly fivefold, grain consumption nearly tripled, fossil fuel burning nearly quadrupled, and air and water pollutants multiplied severalfold. The unfortunate reality is that the economy continues to expand but the ecosystem on which it depends does not, creating an increasingly stressed relationship.

If the economy were to expand only enough to cover population growth until 2050, it would need to grow from the $29 trillion of 1997 to $47 trillion. This, of course, would merely maintain current incomes, unacceptable though they are for much of humanity. If, on the other hand, the economy were to continue to expand at 3 per cent per year, global economic output would reach $138 trillion in the year 2050.

Even the first, more modest, growth projection would likely lead to a deterioration of the Earth's natural systems to the point where the economy itself would begin to decline. It is easy to foresee a scenario of continuing forest destruction, aquifer depletion, and ecosystem collapse that would lead to economic decline. If the world cannot simultaneously convert the economy to one that is environmentally sustainable—one that does not destroy its own support systems—and move to a lower population trajectory, economic decline will be hard to avoid.

24

Taxation System in Developing Countries

There have been radical changes during the last two decades in the academic assessment of the role of governments in economic development. These include the now widely accepted maxim. "As little government as possible as, much as necessary". The degree of government intervention to be discussed is determined by the role of governments. Fiscal policy, as a part of economic policy, is especially affected. Fiscal policy considerations play an equally pivotal role in taking decisions on economic policy in industrial, developing and transition countries alike. For example, this applies when it comes to reducing unemployment, excessive budget deficits and public debt burdens. Or when national savings rates are too low, or governments seek an answer to the problems of pension and public health systems.

Usually, fiscal policy instruments are differentiated as public spending, tax revenue and the budget balance. The following can be implemented as specific fiscal policy activities to influence the economic stability of the transition and growth process; structural taxation reforms; reform of public spending and debt management; extra-budgetary operations; and changes in the less visible, quasi fiscal activities of stateowned enterprises or financial institutions.

The following observations, however, focus on the importance of taxation policy and the institutions needed to implement it. Aspects of public spending and debt management are highlighted only on the sidelines. A brief analysis of the main problem areas in the developing countries will precede reflections on them.

The Developing Countries' Starting-point

Many Asian countries like India made greater efforts in recent years to allocate public funds effectively. They have thereby paid special attention to reforming budget systems and setting priorities for public spending. Changes in the level and structure of public expenditure, such as government investments, subsidies and transfers, can also create general conditions relevant to private sector growth. However, experience in above all the context of structural adjustment programmes shows that successful reform of public budgets also requires reform of the revenue side. Declining budget assistance and low utilisation of existing taxation potential call for a more intensive addressing of the questions of why the public budget is so limited, and how tax-induced economic distortion can be corrected. Summing up, the problems in the government revenue sector can be identified as:

- dependency to taxation on international trade;
- low incomes (subsistence economy, informal sector);
- opaque taxation systems (exemption rules, small tax base, high tax rates);
- lack of economic incentives;
- unequal taxation (unequal treatment of ordinary and judicial people);
- inefficient administrations;
- ponderous administrative procedures;
- hierarchical administrative action;
- low taxpayer honesty;
- political resistance by influential interest groups;
- corruption.

Influence of Taxation Policy on General Economic Development

Taxation policy aspects such as tax structure, design of individual taxes, over-all scope of taxation and taxation administration can in many ways directly influence the allocation of resources, the stability of the economy, and distribution of income, and thus affect growth. Finally, almost every tax provokes a change of behaviour of the economic entity, which leads to wrong allocations and can result in a loss of social services.

Switching from income tax to a tax on consumption, for example, can impact positively on saving behaviour, and thus trigger greater accumulation of capital. Whereas using income as the tax base rewards consumption and penalizes saving (deferred consumption), this does not apply to a tax on personal spending. Empirical studies, however, do not make clear whether the saving level depends on taxation and if so in what form.

Rather, it can be assumed that taxation merely influences the savings structure. Besides that, it must be seen that greater savings do not automatically lead to growth. Using the savings for investments calls for complementary factors such as functioning foreign exchange and finance markets.

Tax incentives such as so-called tax expenditure (which can be offset against tax) to promote investment and R & D can also have a significant influence on allocation of resources and technological progress. The impacts of tax reductions on growth depend on whether and what public spending is cut at the same time. If there are no cuts, the budget deficit can lead to rising interest rates, and thus have a negative influence on growth.

There are reservations with respect to the effectiveness of Tax-induced effects on growth. Equally, social and industrial policy goals such a promotion of investment and R & D are to be questioned. However, developing countries in particular fall back in large measure on the instrument of tax expenditure. Introducing such tax breaks bears the risk that the taxation system will be even more opaque and the tax base eroded. In the case of a given amount of revenue, this results in tax rates for the remaining taxpayers having to be raised. This, in turn, reinforces economic distortions. Moreover, such taxation policy measures can also incur politico-economic costs. They are often accompanied by sinecure-seeking behaviour, corruption and the forming in interest groups, which as a whole can inhibit growth.

Finally, uncertainty over future fiscal or taxation policy can have equally negative impacts on investment and thus growth. Among other things, this can be created by inflationary tendencies or opaque and inconsistent political decision-making processes, which are now customary in many developing countries. Planning security in particular is very important in creating a climate which encourages investment.

On the whole, the international tax reduction competition that goes with globalisation of markets can lead to decreases in growth. The degree to which countries are tempted to attract international customers of foreign capital by cutting taxes and vying with each other in lowering their taxation levels can also refuse revenues and consequently public spending on infrastructure or social services.

A taxation policy aimed at promoting growth should therefore be designed to achieve broadest taxation neutrality. That means tax-induced distortions of resources allocation should be minimised so far as possible in line with given revenue requirements. This can be achieved mainly in the direct taxation sector of income and corporation tax by a distinct reduction of individual tax rates and simultaneous widening of the tax base, extensive scrapping of tax breaks and exemptions, and equal treatment in taxing the government, non-government, private and business sectors. In the developing countries the current taxation method contributes on average only 25-30 per cent of revenue. Essentially, this can be attributed to practical application problems—poor book-keeping and billing, and of the informal sector high proportion of the tax base.

The share of indirect taxation in total revenue is very high in the developing countries. Traditionally, this can be credited to import and export duties. But the price distortions they induce and the heavy dependence of government revenues on external factors such as world trade prices and volumes impact negatively on the countries macroeconomic balance and competitiveness. Consumer taxes in general are characterised by extensive exemptions, taxation at point-of-production, and insufficient registering of the tax base. That is why the taxation system should essentially hinge on a broad tax base that has few exemptions, features indirect taxation in the form of a Value Added Tax on end-consumers, and contains only a few traditional purchase taxes.

It should be emphasised, however, that precisely in developing countries, the design of a taxation system must guarantee a minimum degree of social justice. This can be achieved, for example, by exempting minimum degree of social justice. This can be achieved, for example, by exempting minimum wages or reducing the VAT rate on daily necessities. A regressive taxation effect is to be avoided.

A consistent taxation system, equal taxation, and a stable political situation are essential prerequisites in developing countries for establishing a taxation that is as neutral and predictable as possible, creates an investment friendly climate, and at the same time guarantees the financing of important government services.

These guidelines for a taxation policy targeted on economic growth are in most cases followed only insufficiently in developing countries. Typically, as already mentioned, their taxation systems taxpayers and administrations. Designers of reforms should also are characterised by a high degree of complexity and opaqueness, low tax yields, and hostility between bear in mind whether the available government institutions are able to enforce them. In many developing countries, that calls for a simple taxation system which focuses on indirect taxation and pay-as-you-earn (PAYE) tax, and thus takes account of the poor capacity of the implementing institutions.

Importance of the Implementing Institutions

A consistent material taxation law aligned on the market economy does not inevitably lead to an improved fiscal policy situation in many developing countries. The economic policy objectives laid down in the taxation laws can be successfully implemented only if the people and taxation administration are willing and able to apply the laws.

For this reason, taxation reform must take account of local conditions such as the communication infrastructure and capacity of the administration. Only in this way can it be guaranteed that planned changed are really also applied. Problems of a lack of training, opaqueness of administrative action, and corruption can result in the intended political objectives being counteracted in implementation. Extensive reforms of taxation policy and the budgetary and public spending side have been undertaken in recent years. But studies have proven that reforms were successful only in those countries in which the appropriate organisational, staff and material prerequisites for implementing them were in place, and a comprehensive reform approach was selected.

In this sense, linking taxation policy and tax administration, and public spending and budget systems, in developing and transition countries has a special importance. This finding is also supported by experience in the context of stabilisation and structural adjustment programmes of the IMF and World Bank. Un-realistic assessment of administrative capacities was one of the main causes of the failure of many taxation policies in developing countries. An orderly administration that is based on legal foundations and renounces arbitrary action is of decisive importance for creating a climate for promoting development in the private sector.

The inefficiency of taxation administrations can have various causes. On the one hand, they can be due to taxation law, and on the other hand the taxation administration itself can be at fault because it often lacks resources, professional staff and a clear strategy. This is aggravated by the fact that as a government revenue collection authority, the taxation administration is especially at risk to corruption. And that, differing from culture to culture, can be very marked.

Experience shows that regardless of a country's culture, the efficiency of taxation administration can be improved if the right country-specific incentives and institutions are employed and established, and administrative reform is sure of open and durable political support.

The poor capacities of administrations frequently result in a lack of efficiency and effectiveness in tax collection.

That means the available tax potential is insufficiently utilised. The main causes are:

- inefficient organisational structures and processes;
- lack of know-how within the administrations;
- insufficient registration of taxpayers;
- lack of information and monitoring systems;
- lack of acceptance by taxpayers, and often poorly motivated staff.

These negative points are also the key areas of cooperation to strengthen the efficiency of administrations. Questions of the organisation of building administrative capacities and procedures and processes, training, staff leadership, automation, and enlightening taxpayers are the focus. In the context of reform of taxation administrations, value should be placed on tax compliance, such as improving it by effective public relations work and at the same time establishing efficient tax enforcement.

A close meshing of the political and administrative advisory services is necessary to ensure durable and successful reform of the entire taxation system. Doing so will highlight and take account of the feedback effects between taxation policy and taxation administration, which are linked by the material taxation law. They operate in politically sensitive area, and therefore, require special harmonisation with the partners. Successful implementation can be guaranteed only with the necessary will to reform on the side of the partner government. Moreover, reforms in government revenue systems should not be seen in isolation. They should be tied into reform of public spending policy and the budgetary system, as well as trade and monetary policy. Only comprehensive approaches to reform which take account of the interdependencies between the individual political areas can pursue a joint macroeconomic strategy..

25

Population Growth and Housing

Over the past half-century, the world's housing stock has grown roughly in step with population. Yet for more and more people worldwide, adequate and affordable housing remains beyond reach, driving some into substandard dwellings and slums and others onto the street. This situation stands to worsen, for the need for housing worldwide is projected to nearly double over the next 50 years.

Although industrial nations currently occupy a disproportionately large share of the world's households relative to their population, virtually all future growth will occur in developing countries, where housing requirements will more than double by the middle of the twenty-first century. This phenomenal growth results from the potent synergy between population growth and a shift toward fewer people per household—a trend that is especially pronounced where economic growth is rapid.

HABITAT, the United Nations Centre for Human Settlements, has projected housing requirements based on roughly a 30-per cent reduction in people per household over the next 50 years. These figures are purely statistical estimates and do not consider possible checks in housing growth, such as materials or financial constraints, intensified land competition, or increased poverty. Our own projections assume that household size will indeed decrease, as fertility rates drop and as extended families become more rare, but by a more modest 15 per cent.

Over the next 50 years, housing needs in Africa and the Middle East are expected to increase more than threefold, with tremendous gains in the region's most populous nations; demands are to increase 3.5 times in Nigeria and 4.5 times in Ethiopia. Although less dramatic percentage increase are expected in Asia, the doubling of households in the region will require nearly 700 million additional homes by 2050. Still, some countries there, such as Pakistan and neighbouring Afghanistan, will see housing needs increase nearly three and a half times.

The projected growth in housing needs becomes all the more daunting given that rapid population growth—combined with rapid urban growth—has already left a large share of the world's population without adequate housing. HABITAT estimates that at least 600 million urban dwellers and more than 1 billion rural dwellers in Africa, Asia, and Latin America live in housing that is so overcrowded and of such poor quality with such inadequate provision for water, sanitation, drainage, and garbage collection that their lives and their health are continually at risk.

As the supply of housing falls behind demand, the quality of available housing tends to deteriorate. Cheaper, less durable materials, such as scrap metal and cardboard, are substituted for more expensive, weather-resistant materials, such as concrete and wood. Fierce competition in swelling urban areas for desirable land can eliminate all hope of low-income households acquiring plot for housing. As choice of location dwindles, shantytowns and other low—quality settlements develop on marginal land ill suited for housing-in floodplains, on steep hillsides, near garbage dumps or others environmentally risky sites. From New York to Beijing, cities are faced with land and materials constraints even as their populations continue to grow.

At the same time, housing area per person continues to increase in certain nations and among the more affluent segments of other nations, placing additional stress on prime space and building materials. In the United States, Western Europe, and Japan—a nation traditionally known for small dwellings—floor space per person has more than doubled in new single family homes since mid-century. The global disparity in floor space per person—Washington, D.C., at the high end with 70 square metres per person, and most of humanity at around

9 square metres per person—will likely mimic the growing global disparity in income, as wealthy household scale up and poorer households fill up.

Housing can provide a connection to a supply of fresh water and sanitation facilities. But as its quality deteriorates, so do these basic amenities. Half the world's people are without access to sanitation and nearly this many — 2.7 billion—are without a reliable source of safe drinking water. Shortage of housing that provides these basic services are most acute in cities, where rapid urbanisation and high population densities place heightened demands on infrastructure. And still housing needs are projected to so are in the regions of the world where access to water and sanitation are most constrained.

The ultimate manifestation of population growth outstripping the supply of housing is homelessness. The United Nations estimates that a least 100 million of the world's people-roughly the same as the population of Mexico have no home; the number tops 1 billion if those with especially insecure or temporary accommodations, such as squatters, are included. In many developing countries, squatter communities are home to 30-60 per cent of the urban population. There are some 250, 000 pavement dwellers in Bombay alone. Humans who are born, live, and die in the streets—are common in all major cities. Unless the world moves to a lower population trajectory, the ranks of homeless are likely to swell dramatically.

26

Opening Markets for Agriculture

While the Uruguay Round made a good start—more was done to liberalize agricultural trade and to bring agriculture into the system than in all previous rounds combined—we have to recognize that agriculture still has a long way to go to complete its reform and to be fully integrated into the world trading system. Prior to the Uruguay Round, agricultural trading rules were not in concert with other sectors. The Uruguay Round Agreement (URAA) made good first steps toward bringing agriculture into conformity with international trade rules governing other goods, but much remains to be done.

The Uruguay Round, of course, required certain reductions in trade-distorting measures, and the implementation of those reforms has proceeded very well. Two other legacies of the Uruguay Round are very important for the new negotiations—a mandate to continue what was begun, and a structure for achieving liberalisation. The WTO's "built-in" agenda includes agriculture. It was recognised from the outset that the first period of reform that we are still implementing was only a down payment.

In addition to the commitment to continue negotiations, the URAA—focusing on export subsidies, market access, and domestic support—established a structure on which to build. Establishing a three-pillar structure was the most time-consuming undertaking in the round. Fortunately, we do not need to reinvent that wheel. The structure of the rules provides a logical approach for the negotiations, one which most seem to agree we should keep and build on.

Export Competition

Export subsidies are an illegitimate policy instrument, a symptom of a systemic imbalance in a nation's agricultural policies, the costs of which are borne by others. The costs of domestic policy choices should be borne by the country that chooses them, not foisted onto its trading partners by subsidizing exports. The Uruguay Round made a start at eliminating agricultural export subsidies: 36 per cent reduction of budget expenditures on export subsidies and 21 per cent reduction of quantities over a six-year implementation period. With experience to show that markets adapt, we should now be able to improve the pace of export subsidy reductions and eliminate the export subsidy scourge from agricultural trade. Export subsidies are not allowed in the WTO rules for any other industry. Their use constitutes a source of trade distortion and degradation to the environment, and there is no valid reason to keep them any longer.

Market Access

The Uruguay Round progress on market access leaves much to be done. It left tariffs too high, and it did not create much new market access. The average non-agricultural tariff is now 4 percent, while the average agricultural tariff is over 40 per cent, and tariffs on some products exceed 300 per cent. With a few exceptions, nontariff barriers were converted to tariffs, and members were required to open up at least a small minimum access—3 per cent of domestic consumption initially, growing to 5 per cent by the end of the adjustment period—under tariff-rate quotas.

The stage has been set for real reforms. Let access continue to grow and let all tariffs be reduced to a negotiated maximum level by the end of the transition period. In addition, an examination of the administration of tariff-rate quotas should lead to transparent and open systems.

Many WTO members note that importers were required to change nontariff barriers to tariffs and grant access, while no reciprocal disciplines were imposed on export restraints of exporting countries. Net food importing countries should be able to expect that if they open their border to international market, those international markets will deliver supplies as reliably to importers as to the domestic markets of exporters. Willingness on the part of leading exporting members to discipline export controls will reassure "food security" countries that expanding market access is not risky.

Domestic Support

The Aggregate Measure of Support was a success as a component of the Agreement on Agriculture and the insistence on reducing trade-distorting measures. The drive toward decoupled support ("green box") is the key. By the end of 1996, the United States had largely decoupled farm programmes so that payments to farmers were not linked to a requirement to produce. Other WTO members will also succeed in orienting their policies toward market signals. In the new round, further review and decreases in the aggregate measure of support will clearly lead to market-based agricultural trade.

A new buzzword that some countries are using to justify domestic support is "multi functionality" It is a buzzword for what everybody in agriculture has known for thousands of years: agriculture serves other purposes besides producing food and fibre. But the real problem with the discussion of multi-functionality is not semantic. It is the confusion between policy goals and policy instruments. If the United State appears skeptical about the implications of multi-functionality for WTO rules, the U.S. objection is not multi-functionality as a factual matter. Each country chooses social objectives for themselves. There is no inherent connection between those objectives and trade distorting agricultural policies.

New Issues

While the Uruguay Round established effective disciplines in traditional problem areas, such disciplines have not yet been established in some new areas. As monopolies, state trading enterprises (STEs) can distort trade, and they frequently operate behind a veil of secrecy. The agricultural trading system has much to gain from WTO disciplines on STEs because they allow some countries to undercut exports based on open market transactions and restrict imports.

Biotechnology holds tremendous promise globally for food consumers, producers, and the environment. With the world's population growing by about 2 per cent annually, there are 80 million more mouths to feed each year. Some countries threaten to adopt policies regarding the importation and planting of bio-engineered crops and the labeling of products containing bio-engineered foods that are not based on scientifically justified principles. If our farmers are to meet the challenge of feeding an ever-increasing population with a sustainable agricultural system, then they must have access to the new bio-engineeed varieties. We need to think about how the WTO can help facilitate this new technology.

Developing Countries

One of the critical components to a successful new round of negotiations will be the full participation of a substantially increased number of developing countries. Open trade in agriculture relieves farmers in developing countries of the burden imposed by protectionism and export subsidies, while reducing hunger and offering reliable supplies of food at reasonable prices.

27

Is Copyright on the Wrong Track?

What is the purpose of intellectual property rights? originally they were based on the principle that creators should be granted exclusive rights to exploited their works, in order to ensure they were properly remunerated and, in addition, to encourage creative activity. But in the interest of the community and of future artists and inventors, those exclusive rights were limited in time: when the term of protection ran out, the work fell into the public domain, a copyright-free space that encourages creation and completition. They could than be used as raw material and a kind of "suggestion box" by fresh generations of creators. A balance between the protection of individual property and the general interest was guaranteed.

Today that balance has been destroyed. The founding principles of intellectual property seem to be threatened by an ill-considered increase in the number of privately hald exclusive rights at the expense of the public domain.

Counterfeit Software and Designer Clothes

The main factor hastening these developments is a change in the economy, which focuses increasingly on products with "intellectual added value", such as new software, the selection and presentation of information, specialised computer services, cultural and entertainment products, biotech products, and other applications of cutting-edge technologies. Control of ideas, forms, images and brands is a crucial element in this so-called "immaterial economy".

While it is difficult to steal a consignment of steel girders or a cargo of bananas, it is child's play to copy software or manufacture counterfeit designer clothes. It is easy for intellectual added value to be illicitly appropriated: it cannot be "put under lock and key". Those who want to exploit it for their own profit simply need to be able to reproduce it. Pirates in this field can market copied products at a lower price than the originals, since they do not have to pay the cost of creating or advertising the product. By doing this, they distort competition.

International Negotiations

To protect their industries against piracy and counterfeiting, the member countries of GATT (General Agreement of Tariffs and Trade, which governed international trade from 1947 to 1994) set out to strengthen intellectual property rights within the GATT framework. GATT's main concern was to protect companies from unauthorised copying and unfair competition, thus ensuring they would get a return on their investment.

When GATT concluded its first agreements, intellectual property was not very high on the agenda. In the immediate postwar years, products put on the market still consisted of atoms of matter, not bytes. It was not until the Uruguay Round of talks started in 1986 that the issue came to be discussed at the international level. That round of talks resulted in the signing, on April 15 1994, of the agreement on Trade Related Aspects of Intellectual Property Rights (TRIPS). Like the multilateral agreements on trade in goods, the tax was included in an appendix to the Marrakesh framework agreement that set up GAAT's successors, the World Trade Organisation (WTO).

TRIPS, which has a global application (most countries in the world have now subscribed to it), confirmed the economic importance of intellectual property rights. It requires member states to protect all forms of creation: literal and artistic work in the broadest sense (including maps and press photos). Computer programmes, data bases, sound recordings, radio and television broadcasts, drawings and models, inventions of products and processes in every technological field, the lay-out designs of integrated circuits, and so on.

The agreement was a milestone in the history of intellectual property. First, its scope of application is unprecedentedly wide:

anything created in the fields of technology, software, news or culture can and must be protected by an intellectual property right, in such a way that it exclusively benefits rights holders, who alone decide how it should be reproduced and distributed. Secondly, for the first time TRIPS requires contracting states to organize procedures and sanctions that enable rights holders to ensure that their rights are respected. Those states are for examplc obliged to allow persons or companies, whose rights have been infringed upon to go court and obtain damages. Such duties are chiefly incumbent upon the developing countries. Most of these countries do not possess the human of financial resources that would enable them to develop their own production, and they have tended to become the preferred locations of the copying industries.

A New Right to Protect Investment

Final interests again have prompted to consider the adoption of a directive on the protection of biotechnological inventions. The move was motivated by two factors: first, "the protection of biotechnological inventions will certainly be of key importance for the Community's industrial development", secondly, "research and development, notably in the field of genetic engineering, require a considerable degree of high-risk investment which cannot be profitable unless there is adequate legal protection".

Financial terminology—talk of profitability and an attractive "return on investment"—is invading the sphere of intellectual property. The notion of intellectual property used to be a way of protecting intellectual added value; it has now become an instrument for turning invested capital to good account. Is this a necessity or is it regrettable? The question is worth debating.

It is true that in the field of biotechnology, for example, creation requires considerable investment. This is something that industrial companies cannot accept unless they are sure of being able to make it at least partially profitable. On the other hand, one may reasonably wonder whether there is any point in creating a new monopoly information contained in data bases, even if a great deal of time and money has gone into creating them. The idea here is not to reward an intellectual creation, however slight, but merely to repay an investment in time and money. This trend could well jeopardize the sharing of knowledge. The notion on intellectual property here seems to have departed from its basic purpose, which was to ensure a balance between private and public interests.

This change of direction is one of the first perverse effects of the exponential increase in the amount of space occupied by intellectual property. More fundamentally, it has been engineered by a society that tends to make legal and material protection the keystone of its ethos; all property and anything else of value needs to be protected against risk. Accident prevention, security, insurance and protection have become mantras in developed Western societies. It has reached the point where those societies sometimes seem to have forgotten that risk is an inherent aspect of life and freedom.

The second perverse effect of the boom in intellectual property—the broadening of its scope as well as of its duration—is equally worrying.

On many occasions over the last ten years, legislators and courts have also agreed to an unlimited extension of the scope of copyright protection. Originally designed to protect works of art, copyright has been extended to cover every sphere to human creation, from the design of car bodywork or ties, meteorological photographs and the instruction manuals of electrical household appliances to data bases and receipts. Since everything belongs to someone, an authorisation from the owner is required for everything. In practice it has become extremely difficult to create a multimedia work, to shoot a film, to compose a piece of music, or to publish an illustrated book without in someway having to use elements that are protected by copyright, and therefore having to request a detailed authorisation from copyright holders and to pay them financial compensation.

In the short term, this increase in the number of exclusive rights will be a threat to economic activity itself. Competition, after all, boils down to offering the same product as someone else. Now if that product and all its variants, versions and components are protected by intellectual copyright, copying—

in order words, making a competing offer—becomes an extremely hazardous exercise. If limited exclusive rights, which used to form part of the original spirit of intellectual property, protect companies against illicit copying, disproportionate exclusive rights quite simply wipe out competition altogether.

As for the extension of the duration of copyright, it means that the community's right to make free use of a work after it has fallen into the public domain will be a theoretical possibility rather than a fact. The present duration of copyright protection often exceeds the period during which the created work is in fact usable. After 70 years or more, an old computer programme is of no use to any one.

Similarly, the European directive on data bases theoretically restricts their protection period to 15 years. But it stipulates that if a data base is modified, notably by a large number of additions, deletions or changes which show there has been substantial further investment, the duration can be extended by 15 years. Thus, a regularly updated data base can be protected for ever and will therefore never fall out of copyright. That contravenes the most fundamental principles that underlay the notion of intellectual property rights.

28

For a Fair Sharing of Time

Women may have entered public life on a massive scale, but they are still on their own when it comes to running the household. A new balance must be struck if there is to be genuine democracy. At the dawn of the 21st century, states and the international community can no longer refute the fact that humanity is made up of two sexes, not just one. This discovery, a precious legacy of the century that just closed, has brought women's existence into the limelight. One of the great democratic challenges for societies over the next century will be to mature so that both sexes are able to live their lives on an equal footing, with all their differences, contrasting history and culture, but also with equal rights and responsibilities.

Women's rise to power and their participation in politics are the vital signs of a healthy democracy. If only this vision that emerged from the 1995 Beijing Women's Conference could spread wordwide! one can call it a radicalisation of democracy. When women take part in the public arena, contributing to the ongoing, shared effort to shape better ways of living together, a qualitative leap occurs. Their participation fills a gap which has until now prevented the emergence of a truly democratic culture.

Archaic Attitudes

But attitude are not the only obstacle to women's ambitions. The structure of society and the way men and women run their daily lives are other stumbling blocks. The Inter-American Development Bank has had the good idea of giving the Institute for Cultural Action, and NGO in Rio de Jeneiro, the task of setting up a pilot programme to train women for positions of political and social power. Participants include trade union and NGO leaders, key figures from the black and indigenous communities, company executives, civil servants and policymakers.

These women of different ages, educational backgrounds and ethnic origins are all aware of one fact: they are paying a very high price for a social contract that was negotiated when women were in a position of weakness, and agree that this has to change.

Re-mapping the Division Between Public and Private Life

In Rio de Janeiro revealed that there is an urgent need to re-organize the use of time, to strike a new balance between responsibilities and to re-map the division between public and private life. Household task must be recognised as time consuming, socially and economically vital and a serious check on women's ambitions.

Women in positions of power must constantly prove that they can behave like men. They keep quiet about having to look after children, run a household and care for elderly parents. Bringing those issues out into the open would mean admitting "flaws" that men do not have, for the simple reason that they delegate such work to their wives.

By drawing a veil of silence over their home life as if it were something illicit, women are allowing a basic fact to be hidden: the world of work relies on a domestic zone run by them. Women have changed, but the world of work has not and they are reaching the point of exhaustion. Filled with a deep sense of injustice, they are asking themselves. "Where did I go wrong?"

Understanding that humanity is composed of two different but equal sexes has several implications. Society must redefine itself because women are turning up in public carrying children in their arms and breast-feeding them, and because they have their own awareness and language that come from life experiences which are different from those of men.

An Untenable Double Burden

Articulating issues affecting public and private life is complicated, but that does not mean the equation is impossible of that the problems they raise should be brushed aside especially since the two worlds of public and private life are intertwined and mutually supportive. The balance between the two has now been upset. Women have entered public life on a massive scale, but the organisation of home life how time is used and who is responsible for what tasks is still the same, as if nothing had changed. And yet such a world, where women are expected to soldier on just as before, "simply" adding to their lives experiences hitherto reserved to men, is called egalitarian.

That misunderstanding is fueled by an age-old tradition of dismissing the world of women, even by women themselves. Because society does not consider what they do in the home as having any major social significance, it fails to add this part of their lives to the other side of the equation.

This is why the massive migration of women from the home to the public arena is occurring without societies having to think seriously about how and by whom domestic work will be done in the future (and which women still do, but at what cost!). The double burden, resulting from an out dated social contract, is putting women under mounting pressure by speeding up their lives to an untenable pace. We are facing a social problem that society as a whole must solve and not, as many think, a problem that women must settle by working even harder.

As new areas of power open up to women, both sexes must take a fresh look at how they use time. Re-arranging it is a challenge to society's imagination. But has this necessity sunk into the minds of decision-makers? I do not thank so. This poses a major problem because it is a missing building block in the construction of our democracies.

The everyday work is proof of this. Women must put these issues on the political and economic agenda, thereby contributing to a more radical definition of democracy. Feminism's new demand for a different sharing of time also opens debate that goes beyond the interests of women alone. In the final analysis, time and its constants define the limits of our own lives and the range of choices we make, in accordance with the meaning we give to our own existence.

The equality equation is increasingly complex. It is not enough to wipe out the last traces of discrimination in public life. A new definition of equality will emerge when both sexes start sharing responsibility in the private realm. Otherwise, the issue will be distorted and women will lose all chance of succeeding in public life.

29

Richer or Poorer?

Achievements and Challenges of Ethical Trade

Ethical trade as an approach to supply chain management has mushroomed in recent years. Northern companies are becoming increasingly concerned with the 'ethics' of their operations and risks to reputation and productivity posed by bad employment practices in global supply chains. But can voluntary private sector codes really improve employment conditions in supply chains?

Ethical trade is one dimension of corporate social responsibility, bringing social issues into the mainstream of commercial supply chain management through the use of codes of conduct. It is sometimes confused with fair-trade which addresses terms of trading for smaller producers, and fosters greater responsibility in supply chain relations.

Ethical trade, on the other hand, focuses on workplace issues, requiring that supplier's in particular meet minimum employment, worker welfare and aspects of human rights standards.

Similar management systems are well established for product safety and environmental issues. Here we focus on the social dimensions of ethical trade and its codes of conduct yet the separation of social and environmental standards is increasingly artificial in global souring agreements. A plethora of codes are on offer. The most numerous are in-houses codes such as Nike's 233 company codes counted in 1999 and the figure is rising.

Suppliers have to comply with and pay for multitude of similar but different codes. Harmonising codes or establishing equivalence is on the agenda but has not yet halted the problem of 'code overload'

At a broader level, industry-specific codes have also been developed. The US Apparel industry Partnership/Fair Labour Agreement adopted by a number of leading US merchandising companies is a good example. Industry standards are not new, as ISO and EMAS environmental management systems show. Building on ISO principles, Social Accountability International (formerly CEPAA) has development SA8000. This is an independent social standard that can be used as an auditable code throughout the private sector.

Ethical trade is partly a response to consumer and campaigning group pressure in globalised economy. Alliances of companies, NGOs, trade. Developing codes of conduct through a multi stakeholder approach is a striking aspect of ethical trade, bringing together companies, NGOs, trade unions and some government departments. An example of this collaborative approach is the Ethical Trading Initiative (ETI) in the UK. The ETI's baseline code of conduct that corporate members from various industries must comply with as a minimum standard is more than just a code, ETI aims to provide a learning environment and sponsors pilot projects in developing countries to test different methods of monitoring and verification.

Codes of conduct need to be assessed in terms of content, implantation and impact. A number of professional auditing companies have moved into this area, some accredited to audit specific codes such as FLA or SA8000. Suppliers audited against a specific code undergo an inspection, and where noncompliance is found, have to take remedial action or risk failing the audit.

Social auditing is a complex process, however, and it can be difficult to spot work place abuse, such as sexual harassment or forced overtime. Workers have little confidence in a process that appears to be linked with management, and fear that reporting issues could risk their jobs. Advocates of the multi stakeholder approach argue that effective monitoring and verification of codes must involve local NGOs and trade unions in which workers have trust. Participatory social auditing also a means of raising awareness and of facilitating behavioural change, can help reveal serious management problems. But in many developing countries local organisations lack the capacity to participate: developing sustainable local systems of monitoring and verification remains an important challenge.

Do the advantages of multi-stakeholder approaches outweight immediate constraints? Ethical trade is a largely northern driven process, reflecting Western ethical thinking and priorities, Southern based initiatives, however, are expanding, raising the possibility of local ownership of codes, Collaboration poses challenges. Stronger relationships and better understanding are essential between southern and northern workers, producers, trade unions, and NGOs for codes to work globally.

But there is still scepticism as to the extent of the benefits that ethical trade might bring. Will increasing southern capacity to participate, as the ETI has done in its pilot project, help? Will building trust, confidence and dialogue achieve the objectives of ethical trade, north and south? Child labour is often more complex, however, than codes make it appear. Codes meet to address the conditions of all workers within the supply chain, including the least visible; partnerships must include all groups to address these limitations.

The role of government is hotly contested. Can a system whose credibility depends on under-resourced civil society actors, often excluding democratically elected representatives, maintain genuine credibility? If the boundaries between private sector and public sector roles are not defined, the list of private sector responsibilities will become unmanageable. Private sector initiatives are not a substitute for more comprehensive national or international development policies.

What are the consequences of codes? Do they encourage downsizing or reinforce from large suppliers where compliance is more easily monitored? There is a risk that the gains of some will be at the expense of others.

Ethical trade has successfully begun forging partnerships to find solutions. While it might be wrong to assume that ethical trade can change the world, handled wisely it could make a world of difference for some. Yet it is not a panacea for development. Issues that remain unchallenged by ethical trade include:

- The exclusion of companies producing for domestic markets—often bigger employers.
- Underlying causes of poverty and social marginalisation.

Bibliography

Ackoff, R.L., *Redesigning the Future: A System Approach to Societal Problems* (John Wiley, 1974).

Adelman, I., et. al. *Economic Growth and Social Equality in Developing Countries* (California, Standford University, 1967).

Aggarwal, Y.P., *Education and Human Resource Development* (New Delhi, Commonwealth, 1988).

Amirk Singh., 'New Policy on Education: Two Years Later', *Economic & Political Weekly,* Special Number, Vol. XXIII, Nos. 45, 46 & 47, pp. 2479-92.

Anand, Mulk Raj, 'A Nation of Illiterates' *The Tribune*. Feb. 12, 1991.

Anderson, C.A., 'A Skeptical Note on Education and Mobility', A.H. Halsey, & Others (ed)—*Education Economy and Society,* (New York, The Free Press, 1969), pp. 164-182.

Anderson, C.A., 'Access to Higher Education and Economic Development' in *Halsey, A.H. (Ed)-op. cit.* Work. pp. 252-268.

Anderson, C.A. and Bowman, M.J., *Education and Economic Development* (Chicago, 1965).

Anon, *'The Pressure of Economic Change'* in A.H. Halsey, (Ed), *op. cit.* pp. 22-30.

Anon, 'All-out Bid to Tap Human Resources', *The Economic Times* (Supplement), Dec. 20, 1984, pp. 1-3.

Asharaya, P., 'Education: Politics and Social Structure', *Economic and Political Weekly,* Vol. XX, No. 42, Oct. 19, 1985, pp. 1785-89.

Bantock, G.A. *Education and Values,* (London, Faber and Faber, 1966).

Bauer, R.A. (Ed), *Social Indicators* (Cambridge and London, MIT Press, 1966).

Becker, Garry S., *Human Capital* (Princeton, Princeton University Press, 1964).

Becker, Garry, S., *Human Capital: A Theoretical and Empirical Analysis with Special Reference to Education,* (New York, NBER, 1974).

Ben-Porath, Yoram. 'The Production of Human Capital and the Life Cycle of Earnings', *The Journal of Political Economy,* August, 1967, pp. 352-65.

Benson, Charles S. *Perspectives on the Economic of Education* (Boston, Houghton Mifflin Company, 1963).

Bhalla, G.S. and Bhalla, H.S. 'Human Resource Development for Rural Poor', Paper presented at the *U.G.C. National Seminar,* held at G.K. I. A.S. in Rural Development, Punjab University, Campus, Damdama Sahib).

Bhatia, S.K., 'Challenge in Human Resource Management', *Indian Management,* Vol. 25, No. 8, August 1986, pp. 5-12.

Blaug, Mark (Ed), *Economics of Education-I* (New York, Penguin, 1968).

Blaug, Mark (Ed), *Economics of Education-II* (New York, Penguin, 1969).

Blaug, Mark, *An Introduction to the Economics of Education* (New York, Penguin, 1970).

Blaug. Mark, 'The Empirical Status of Human Capital Theory: Slightly Jaundiced Survey', *Journal of Economic Literature,* Vol. 14, No.3, September 1976, pp. 827-55.

Boulding, K., *The Meaning of the Twentieth Century* (London Allen, & Unwin, 1965).

Bowman, M.J., 'Education and Economic Growth *in King, I (Ed), Education and Income* (Staff Working Paper No. 402, Washington, World Bank, 1980) pp. 1-71.

Bowman, M.J., 'The Human Investment Revolution in Economic Thought', *Sociology of Education* 39/2 (Spring), pp. 111-37.

Brown, Murraya (Ed), *The Theory and Empirical Analysis of Production* (New York, NBER, 1967).

Brownstein, L., *Education and Development in Rural Kenya* (New York, Praeger, 1972).

Burgess, T., et al., *Manpower and Educational Development in India* (London, Oliver & Boynd).

Byars, L.L. & Rue, L. W., *Human Resorce Management* (Illinois, Irwin Homewood).

Chattopadhyay, G., 'Education: The Authority to Learn or the Authority of the Bowl of Hemlock' in *Decision* (IIM, Calcutta), Vol. 16, No. 1, Jan-March, 1989, pp. 22-33.

Cheema, C.S. 'The Challenges of Human Resorce Development in Rural Punjab'—Paper presented at *U.G.C. National Seminar* held at G.K.I.A.S. in Rural Development, Punjabi University Campus, Damdama Sahib).

Clark, Harold F., 'The Return on Educational Investment' in C.S. Benson, (Ed), *op. cit.,* 1963, pp. 24-32.

Coombs, P.H. and Manzoor Ahmed, *Attacking Rural Poverty: Non-Formal Education Can Help* (John Hopkins University Press, 1974).

Coombs, P.H., *The World Crisis in Education: The View from Eighties* (Oxford, OUP, 1985).

Correa, Hector, *The Economics of Human Resources* (Amsterdam, North-Holland, 1963).

Crule, Adam, 'Some Aspects of Educational Planning in Underdeveloped Areas, *Harvard Educational Review*, Vol. 32, No. 3, 1962.

D' Souza, A.A. and De Souza., A. *Population Growth and Human Development* (Delhi, ISI, 1974).

Datta, S., 'Human Resource Development', *Man and Development*, Vol. 8, No. 1, March 1986, pp. 9-17.

Davis, R.G., *Planning Human Resource Development*, (Chicago, 1966).

Davis, Russel G. *Planning Human Resoruce Development: Education Models and Schemata* (Chicago, CSED, Harvard University, 1966).

Denison, Edward F., 'Education and Growth' in Benson, C.S (Ed), *op. cit.*, pp. 33-42.

Desai A. R. *Social Background of Indian Nationalism* (Bombay, Popular, 1966).

Deshmukh, C.D. 'Management and Administration: New Trends', *Training Abstracts 17*, New Delhi Training Division, 1972.

Dey, B., 'On Costing Education' in Pandit's *Measurement of Cost Productivity and Efficiency of Education* (New Delhi, NCERT, 1969), pp. 14-26.

Dey, B. 'Training in the Civil Services: Plea for A Holistic Construal', *Indian Journal of Public Administration* Vol. XXIV, No. 4, Oct.-Dec. 1982.

Drucker, Peter F. 'The Educational Revolution' in Halsey and others (Ed) *op, cit.*, pp. 15-21.

Druker, Peter, F., *Managing in Turbulent Times* (William Heinemann, 1980).

Dwivedi, R.S., *Management of Human Resources: A Behavioural Approach to Personal* (New Delhi, Oxford & IBH, 1982).

Farooq, Khan A., 'Development of Human Resources', *The Economic Times*, September 22, 1984.

Gandhi, Rajiv, 'New National Policy on Education', *Inaugural Address* at the Conference of Education Ministers at New Delhi, August 29,1985.

Gill K.S., 'Agricultural Development in Punjab' in Johar and Khanna's (Ed), *Studies in Punjab Economy* (Amritsar, GNDU, 1983).

Gore, M.S., 'Literacy: Equaliser of Opportunity', *Democratic World*, March 31, 1991, Vol. XX, No. 13.

Gostkowski, Z. *Towards A System of Human Resources Indicators for Less-Developed Countries* (The Polish Academy of Sciences).

Government of India, *Challenges of Education: A Policy Perspective* (Government of India, Ministry of Education 1985)

Government of India, *National Policy on Education* (New Delhi Govt. of India, 1986).

Government of India, *National Policy on Education: Programme of Action* (New Delhi, Govt. of India, 1986).

Groves, Harold M., 'Education and Economic Growth' in C.S. Benson, (Ed), *op, cit.*, pp. 7-11.

Halsey, A.H. and others (Ed), *Education, Economy and Society* (New York, The Free Press, 1969).

Harbison, F., 'The Prime Movers of Innovations' in Halsey, A.H. & Others (Ed) *op. cit.*

Harbison, F. *Human Resources as the Wealth of Nations* (London, OUP, 1973).

Harbison, F. and Myers, C.A. *Education, Manpower and Economic Growth* (New York, 1974).

Havighurst, R.J., 'Education and Social Mobility' in Four Societies' in A.H. Halsey, & others (Ed), *op. cit.*, pp. 105-120.

Heyneman, S.P., *Improving the Quality of Education in Developing Countries* (Washington, World Bank, 1983).

Heyneman, S.P. and White, D.S., *The Quality of Education and Economic Development* (Washington, World Bank, 1986).

Hicks, Norman, *Economic Growth and Human Resources*, World Bank, Staff Paper No. 408, (Washington, World Bank, 1980).

Hilton School of. *Human Resource Development* (Vellore, ISSR, 1989).

Huq. M.S., *Education, Manpower and Development in South and South-East Asia* (Delhi, Sterling, 1975).

Hussian, Majid, *Agricultural Geography* (New, Delhi, Inter-India, 1986).

Jagannathan, N., 'Gender Equality in Education', *University News*, Vol. XXIX, No. 5, Feb. 4, 1991, pp. 1-5.

Jamison, D.T. and Laurence, J.L., *Farmer Education and Farm Efficiency* (Baltimore, John Hopkins, 1982).

Jhingan, M.L., *The Economics of Development and Planning* (New Delhi, Vikas, 1975).

Johnson, D. Gale., 'Economics and the Education System, in C.S. Eenson, (Ed), *op. cit.*, pp. 374-80.

Joshi, P.C. 'Role of Culture in Social Transformation and National Integration, *Economic & Political Weekly*, Vol. XXI, No. 28.

Kamat, A.R., *Progress of Education in Rural Maharashtra* (Pune, Gokhale Institute of Politics and Economics, 1968).

Khanna, G., Parkash, S. and Bansal, R.K., *Unit Cost of College Education in Punjab* (Patiala, Punjabi University, 1985) Mimeo.

Khullar, K.K., 'Four Decades of Education', *Yojana*, Vol. 33, No. 8. Nov. 1-15, 1989, pp. 12-4.

King, T. (Ed)., *Education and Income,* World Bank Staff Working, Paper No. 402, (Washington, World Bank 1980).

Kirpal, P. 'How to Plan Education of the Future', *Yojana,* Vol. 33, No. 14 and 15, August, 1989.

Kothari, Commission, *Report of the Education Commission:* 1964-66 (Delhi, Government of India, 1970).

Kothari, V. N. and Panchamukhi, P.R., 'Economics of Education: A Trend Report' in *ICSSR's A Survey of Research in Economics* (New Delhi, 1980) pp. 169-238.

Krishnamurthy, H.V. 'Human Resource Development Strategy for 21st Century; *P.U. Managemnt Review,* Vol. 9, Nos. 1 and 2, Jan-Feb. 1986, pp. 79-89.

Kulkarni, V.G. 'Alternatives in Education' *Man and Development* (Vol. VIII), March 1985, pp. 25-58.

Lipton, *Why Poor Stay Poor: A study of Urban Bias in World Development* (London, Templesmith, 1977).

MacNamara, R.S. *The Assualt on World Poverty* (Washington, World Bank, 1975).

Mahajan, V.S. 'Whither National Policy: Education', *The Tribune,* Feb, 24,1991, p.8.

Majumdar, Tapas. *Investment in Education and Social Choice,* (New York, Cambridge University Press, 1983).

Marshall, Alfred. 'Education and Invention' in Benson, C.S. (Ed), *op. cit.,* pp. 82-83.

Mathur, B.L. (Ed)., *Human Resource Development: Strategic Approaches and Experiences,* (Jaipur, Arihant, 1989).

Mathur, R.N., *Population Analysis and Studies* (Allahabad, Chugh).

Megginson, L.C., *Personnel and Human Resource Administration,* 1974.

Mehta, M.M., *Human Resource Development Planning,* (Delhi, Macmillan, 1976).

Mingat, Alan and Tan, Jee-Pang. *Analytical Tools for Sector Work in Education* (Baltimore London, John Hopkins University Press, 1988).

Mishra, L. 'Literacy: Now or Never' in *Yojana,* Vol. 34, No. 20, Nov. 1-5, 1990, pp. 4-5.

Misra, S.K. and Puri, V.K., *Development and Planning: Theory and Practice,* (Bombay, Himalaya, 1986).

Moddie, A.D. *Explorations in Management Development* (New Delhi, AIMA, 1976).

Myrdal, G., *Asian Drama* (Penguin, 1963).

Nadler, L., *Developing Human Resources* (Texas, Concepts, 1979).

Nadler, L., *The Handbook of Human Resources Development* (John Willey, 1984).

Nallagounden, A.M. 'Investment in Education in India' *Journal of Human Resource,* Vol. 2, No. 3, Summer-1967, pp. 347-58.

Nandedker, V.G., 'Human Resource: Both an End and Means', *Yojana,* Vol. 34, Nos. 1 and 2, Jan. 26, 1990, pp. 50-53.

National Council of Educational Research and Training. *The Fourth All India Education Survey* (New Delhi, NCERT, 1982).

Niland, John R., *The Production of Manpower Specialists: A Volume of Selected Papers* (New York, Cornell University, 1971).

Nurkse, R., *Problems of Capital Formation in Underdeveloped Countries,* (New Delhi, OUP, 1973).

OECD, *Education in OECD Developing Countries: Trends and Perspectives,* (France, OECD, 1974).

Ota, Masao. 'Quantitative Method for the Planning of Human Resource Development', *Research Bulletin of the National Institute for Educational Research,* No. 11, 1972, pp. 25-41.

Panchamukhi, V.R. Leading Issues in Human Resource Development in India' in P.R. Brahmananda, and V.R. Panchamukhi, (Ed), *Development Process of the Indian Economy,* (Bombay, Himalaya, 1987), pp. 1060-1108.

Pandit, H.N., *Measurement of Cost Productivity and Efficiency of Education* (Delhi, NCERT, 1969).

Rao, B.S., 'Developing Human Resources in Rural Areas: Some Basic Propositions' in M.K. Rao and P.P Sharma, (Ed), *Human Resource Development for Rural Development* (Bombay, Himalaya, 1989), pp. 3-6.

Rao, N.K. and Sharma, P.P., *Human Resource Development for Rural Development* (Bombay, Himalaya, 1989).

Rao, T.V., 'Some Thoughts on HRD in Education', *Indian Journal of Training and Development* (July -Sept., 1986), pp. 135-7.

Rao, T.V., et al., *Alternative Approaches and Strategies of Human Resource Development* (Jaipur, Rawat, 1988).

Rao, T.V., 'Planning for Human Resources Development' in Mathur B.L. (Ed.), *op. cit*.

Rao, V.L., 'Human Element in Economic Development' in Rao, M.K. and Sharma, P.P. (Ed), *op. cit.*, pp. 20-27.

Rao, V.K. R.V., *Education and Human Resoure Development* (Bombay, Allied 1960).

Ravishankar, S., et al., *Human Resource Development: In a Changing Environment* (Bombay, Dhruv and Deep, 1988).

Raza, Moonis, et al., *Education and the Future: An Indian Perspective,* A UNESCO Sponsored Study (New Delhi NIEPA, 1983).

Raza, Moonis (Ed), *Education Planning; A Long Term Perspective* (Delhi, Concept 1986).

Ruark, Henry C. (jr.), 'Technology and Education' in *Benson, C.S. (Ed), op. cit.*, pp. 381-92.

Sapra, C.L. and Aggarwal, Y. (Ed) *Education in India: Critical Issues* (New Delhi, National, 1987).

Saxena, J.P., *et al.*, 'Human Resource Development Strategy', for India's Seventh Plan', *The Economic Times,* July 25, 1984.

Schelsky, H., 'Technical Change and Educational Consequences', in Halsey (Ed), *op.cit.*, pp. 31-6.

Pandit, H.N., A Study in Unit Costs at School Stage in India: A Design of the Research Project (Pandit, H.N. (Ed), *1969, op. cit., pp.* 3-13.

Panigrahi, D., 'Human Resource Development in Business Administration', B.L. Mathur, (Ed), *op, cit.*

Parkash, Shri., *Educational System of India:* An Econometric Study (Delhi, Concept, 1978).

Parminder Kaur, and Singh, Bhawdeep, 'Human Resource Development in Rural Punjab' in *U.G.C. National Seminar* held at G.K.I. A.S. in Rural Development (Punjabi University Campus), Damdama Sahib, 22-23 Feb., 1991.

Patel, S.J., 'Education Mircacle in the Third World', *Economic and Political Weekly,* Vol. XX, No. 31, August 3, 1985, pp. 1312-17.

Patil, V.T. and Patil, B.C., *Problems in Indian Education* (New Delhi, Oxford and IBH, 1982).

Perlman, R., *The Economics of Education: Conceptual Problems and Policy Issues* (Mc Graw Hill, 1973).

Paillai, S. S., 'Educational System and Social Structure', *Educational India,* Vol. 9, March, 1973.

Planning Commission., *The Sixth Five Year Plan:* 1980-85 (New Delhi, Government of India).

Planning Commission., *The First Five Plan: 1951-56* (Delhi, Government of India).

Psachorapoulos, G., *Earnings and Education in OECD Countries* (Paris, OECD, 1973).

Psachorapoulos, G., 'Education and Development—A Review', *Pigmy Economic Review,* Monthly Economic Journal of the Syndicate Bank, Oct. 88, 34, No.3.

Punit, A.E., *Social system in Rural India* (New Delhi, Sterling 1978).

Radhakrishnan, S., *The Creative Life.*

Index